THE BROADWAY LIMITED

by

Joel Rosenbaum and Tom Gallo

A Railpace Company Publication

Photo/Tom Gallo Collection

Famous name trains owe their reputation to the men and women who daily answered the call to duty, be it engine and train service, onboard services, or operations.

The *Broadway Limited* has been served by hundreds of individuals throughout its long history, now in its eighth decade of service. One such individual of note is Joe Szraga.

Joe handled the electrified portion of the *Broadway Limited* between New York and Harrisburg, where he and his GG1 were exchanged for a new engineer and diesels for the run westward to Chicago.

Joe Szraga's railroad career spanned forty three years-- from 1939 to 1983, with the decade 1956-1966 spent operating the *Broadway Limited*. This book is dedicated to Joe Szraga, and all the past and present railroaders involved in making the *Broadway Limited* a great train then.... and a great train today.

Tom Gallo

Joe Szraga   Photo/Tom Gallo Collection

Dedication

THE BROADWAY LIMITED

by

Joel Rosenbaum and Tom Gallo

PUBLISHED BY
RAILPACE COMPANY, INC.
P.O. Box 927
Piscataway, NJ 08855-0927

This publication is available from the publisher at the above address at $18.00 postpaid. NJ residents add 6% sales tax. Also available from leading hobby retailers.

DESIGN AND LAYOUT .... TOM NEMETH
TYPESETTING .... JEAN HILL
COLOR SEPARATIONS .... Litho-Tech, Franklin, NJ
PRINTING .... The Kutztown Publishing Company, Kutztown, PA

Library of Congress Cataloging-in-Publication Data

Rosenbaum, Joel, 1945-
  The Broadway Limited

  1. Broadway Limited (Express Train) 2. Pennsylvania
Railroad. 3. Amtrak. 4. Railroads--United States--Express-trains.
I. Gallo, Tom. II Title.
TF25.P4R67 1988 385'09748 88-32103

ISBN 0-9621541-0-5

Printed and Manufactured in the United States of America
First Printing: November, 1988

COPYRIGHT 1988 RAILPACE COMPANY, INC.

COVER PHOTOGRAPHS

FRONT COVER: Parlor-observation car Mountain View offers a cozy haven for Chicago-bound passengers as it brings up the markers of PRR Train 29, the *Broadway Limited* at Altoona, Pennsylvania 10:25 p.m., October 16, 1966.
Kodachrome/Robert Malinoski

INSIDE FRONT COVER: The *Broadway Limited*, operating as Train 41 under the Amtrak banner, snakes through the famous S-curve in Elizabeth, New Jersey at 5:18 p.m., September 9, 1972. Penn Central GG1's 4899 and 4911 are in charge of the 12 car *Broadway* consist.
Kodachrome/Robert Malinoski

INSIDE REAR COVER: Conrail E8A 4022 leads an A-B-B-A lashup and a 17-car Amtrak *Broadway Limited* consist eastward across the Rockville Bridge in October, 1977. Amtrak Inspection Car 10000 brings up the markers.
Kodachrome/Tom Kelcec

REAR COVER: Pennsylvania E8's 4268 and 4248 lead an eight car eastbound *Broadway Limited* out of Chicago Union Station in September, 1967, only a few months before the Penn Central merger. The view looks north from the Roosevelt Road overpass, a favorite perch for Chicago area trainwatchers and photographers.
Kodachrome/Richard D. Forest

CONTENTS

Dedication 2

Introduction 6

Chapter One: Early History 12

Chapter Two: Birth and Development of the *Broadway Limited* 18

Chapter Three: A Fleet of Modernism: The 1938 Streamlined *Broadway Limited* 32

Chapter Four: The Post-War Years 44

Chapter Five: Amtrak Takes the Throttle 74

References and Acknowledgements 94

Meet the Authors 95

EAST GATE TRACK NINE beckons travelers to board the BROADWAY LIMITED in Pennsylvania Station, New York.   Ektachrome/Tom Gallo

 INTRODUCTION

Mention the name *Broadway Limited* in a group of middle-aged and older railfans, and in their mind will be a flashing streak of Tuscan red Pullmans speeding their way from New York to Chicago. To most people, Broadway evokes images of brightly-lit marquees of the New York theatre district. Yet the Pennsylvania Railroad never had the Great White Way in mind when it renamed its *Pennsylvania Special* in 1912, and *The Broad Way Limited* was in reference to the Pennsylvania's multiple-track right of way over which the train operated.

Some of the larger newspapers of the era immediately began spelling the train's name as though it were one word. With America's fascination by the movies and stage in the 1920's and 1930's, the railroad soon realized that the newspaper misinterpretation of the train's monicker was not such a bad idea. Soon the Pennsylvania Railroad was spelling Broadway the way everyone else does-- as one word. Today, the name *Broadway Limited* still retains a certain exotic and exciting connotation.

A history of the *Broadway Limited* cannot be written without at least due reference to its arch-rival, the New York Central System's *Twentieth Century Limited*. The *Century* and the Pennsy's *Pennsylvania Special* were both inaugurated on the same day, June 15, 1902. Many historians also consider this the birthdate of the *Broadway Limited*.

Booklet issued by the Pennsylvania Railroad for the 1926 Sesqui-Centennial International Exposition at Philadelphia. The illustration touts the Pennsylvania as the "Broad Way" of America's Transportation System, a reference to PRR's multiple-track main lines. It was from this concept that the name *Broad Way Limited* was developed. Joel Rosenbaum Collection

Striking a time-honored pose, observation cars of the *Broadway Limited* and the *Twentieth Century Limited* pause at Englewood, Illinois in 1965. In minutes both trains would arrive their respective terminals in Chicago.
Photo/Jim Boyd

Competition between the two flagship trains of the Pennsylvania and New York Central reached its zenith on June 15, 1938 when streamlined versions of both trains were launched on their thirty-sixth anniversaries. The *Broadway Limited* outlived its competitor as an all-Pullman train by a decade. Only when the Central dropped the name *Twentieth Century Limited* from its timetable in 1967 did the Pennsylvania dare to add coaches to its flagship.

Pennsylvania Railroad
THE STANDARD RAILROAD OF THE WORLD

THE BROADWAY LIMITED, pulled by K2sa 3402 rolls through Elizabeth, New Jersey on July 27, 1913 during the second year of its operation. Note the four-track main line. SMITHSONIAN INSTITUTION Print No. 2223

Rivalry between the two trains became moot after the Pennsy and Central merged in 1968. The Penn Central debacle is history, and passenger service continued to deteriorate rapidly. Only the creation of Amtrak in May, 1971 prevented the complete collapse of the American passenger train. Fortunately, the *Broadway Limited* and its route were selected to be included in Amtrak's final system plan. A Washington section was added to the *Broadway* under Amtrak, and since its inception, the *Broadway Limited* has experienced some interesting route changes.

Now it's time to don our engineer's caps, fit our safety goggles and find a sturdy seat, as we will be hitting speeds up to 127 miles an hour on our historical journey aboard..... *The Broadway Limited.*

This colorful illustration touting the restyled *Broadway Limited* appeared on the rear cover of the June 15, 1938 PRR system passenger timetable. Note credit to Raymond Loewy, master industrial designer responsible for the styling of Pennsy's "Fleet of Modernism".
    Tom Gallo Collection

Above: *Like a smart club, a typical Observation Car.*
Below: *Master Room. Complete private bathroom with shower adjoining.*

A FLEET OF MODERNISM
LED BY A NEW AND FINER
BROADWAY LIMITED

FIRST ALL-ROOM TRAIN IN HISTORY .. NEW FAST TIME

EIGHT premier Pennsylvania trains, four in each direction, now constitute *a Fleet of Modernism*. Designed by Pennsylvania Railroad and Pullman Company engineers in collaboration with Raymond Loewy, noted industrial designer, and led by a new, magnificent ... *Broadway Limited!*

Staffed with valet, barber, manicurist, maid and train secretary, this leader now becomes an all-room Pullman train. A wider range of private accommodations than ever before. Master Rooms, Roomettes, Drawing Rooms, Compartments, Double Bedrooms —all equipped with real beds and individual toilet facilities. Privacy for every passenger! New-style diners, too—excitingly different. Faster schedule also — over the shortest route between east and west.

BROADWAY LIMITED — 16 HOURS !
(Daylight Saving Time)

Lv. New York	6:00 P. M.
Lv. Philadelphia	7:20 P. M.
Ar. Chicago	9:00 A. M.
Lv. Chicago	4:30 P. M.
Ar. Philadelphia	8:09 A. M.
Ar. New York	9:30 A. M.

(DESCRIPTIONS OF OTHER TRAINS OF THE FLEET ON SUCCEEDING PAGES)

ABOVE: The *Broadway Limited* has just clattered across the diamonds at 21st Street, Chicago to begin its eastward journey to New York. Observation-Lounge *Mountain View* brings up the markers on a sunny evening in July, 1966.
Kodachrome/Mike Schafer

LEFT: E units continued to power the Broadway during its first few years of operation under the Amtrak banner. Number 421 leads two sisters, "elephant style" across the diamonds at 21st Street, Chicago on May 9, 1976.
Kodachrome/Preston Cook

LEFT: The Pennsylvania Railroad's Chicago Limited crosses the Susquehanna River on the Rockville Bridge in 1892. The new "fast" train, inaugurated in 1881, cut the running time between New York and Chicago to 26 hours.
E.L. Pardee Collection

BELOW: An early Pennsylvania Railroad buffet car.
E.L. Pardee Collection

Chapter One:

Early History

P.R.R. "Bay Window Car", vintage 1890-1895, was a monument to Victorian elegence with plush divans, armchairs and footstools.

E.L. Pardee Collection

P.R.R. NEW YORK-CHICAGO PULLMAN SERVICE

Enthusiasts of the Pennsylvania Railroad might be surprised to learn that the first sleepers to operate on the Pennsylvania Railroad between Chicago and Jersey City involved connections with the Central Railroad of New Jersey. Through sleeper service began in January 1868 over the Pennsylvania Central, as the Pennsy was then known. The sleepers were switched out at Harrisburg to the Reading for forwarding to the Central Railroad of New Jersey. This gateway to New York was known as the Allentown Route, and in later years this became famous as the route of the Reading-Central RR of New Jersey's *Queen of the Valley* and *Harrisburg Special* passenger trains.

The June 1868 issue of *The Travelers Official Railway Guide*, noted that the Central Railroad of New Jersey 9:00 a.m. *Morning Express* carried Palace sleeping cars through between New York (Jersey City) and Chicago. It was duly noted that the CRR of NJ's *Morning Express* left two hours later than other lines and arrived at principal places in the West at the same time.

In August 1868 another through sleeping car route between New York and Chicago was established, running via Philadelphia on rails of the United Railroad Companies of New Jersey between Philadelphia and Jersey City. This service was initially operated twice a week. In 1871 the United Railroad Companies of N.J. was leased to the Pennsylvania Railroad for 999 years. Control of this route spelled doom for the CRR of NJ/Reading through cars via Harrisburg. On June 30, 1873 Pennsylvania Railroad through car service between Jersey City and the west via the Allentown Route was discontinued. A little more than a century later the Pennsylvania Railroad in the form of Penn-Central would again embrace the CRR of N.J. and the Reading in the homoginization of Eastern railroading known as Conrail.

LEFT: The PRR *Pennsylvania Limited* was re-equipped on January 15, 1898 by the Pullman Palace Car Company. Cars were Brewster green below the window sash and creme yellow above, with red letterboards and decorations in gold. PRR employees affectionately dubbed it the *Yellow Kid*. Train is seen posed at the east end of the Rockville Bridge in 1898 behind D16 4-4-0 174.
SMITHSONIAN INSTITUTION: Print No. 21645

BELOW: Parlor-club-baggage *Cassius* was assigned to the *Pennsylvania Limited*. The Brewster green, creme yellow and red colors of the Mexican flag decorated the Pullman-built private cars of Mexican President Porfirio Diaz, and impressed PRR officials to the extent that they copied the livery for their own *Pennsylvania Limited*.
SMITHSONIAN INSTITUTION: Print No. P4354A

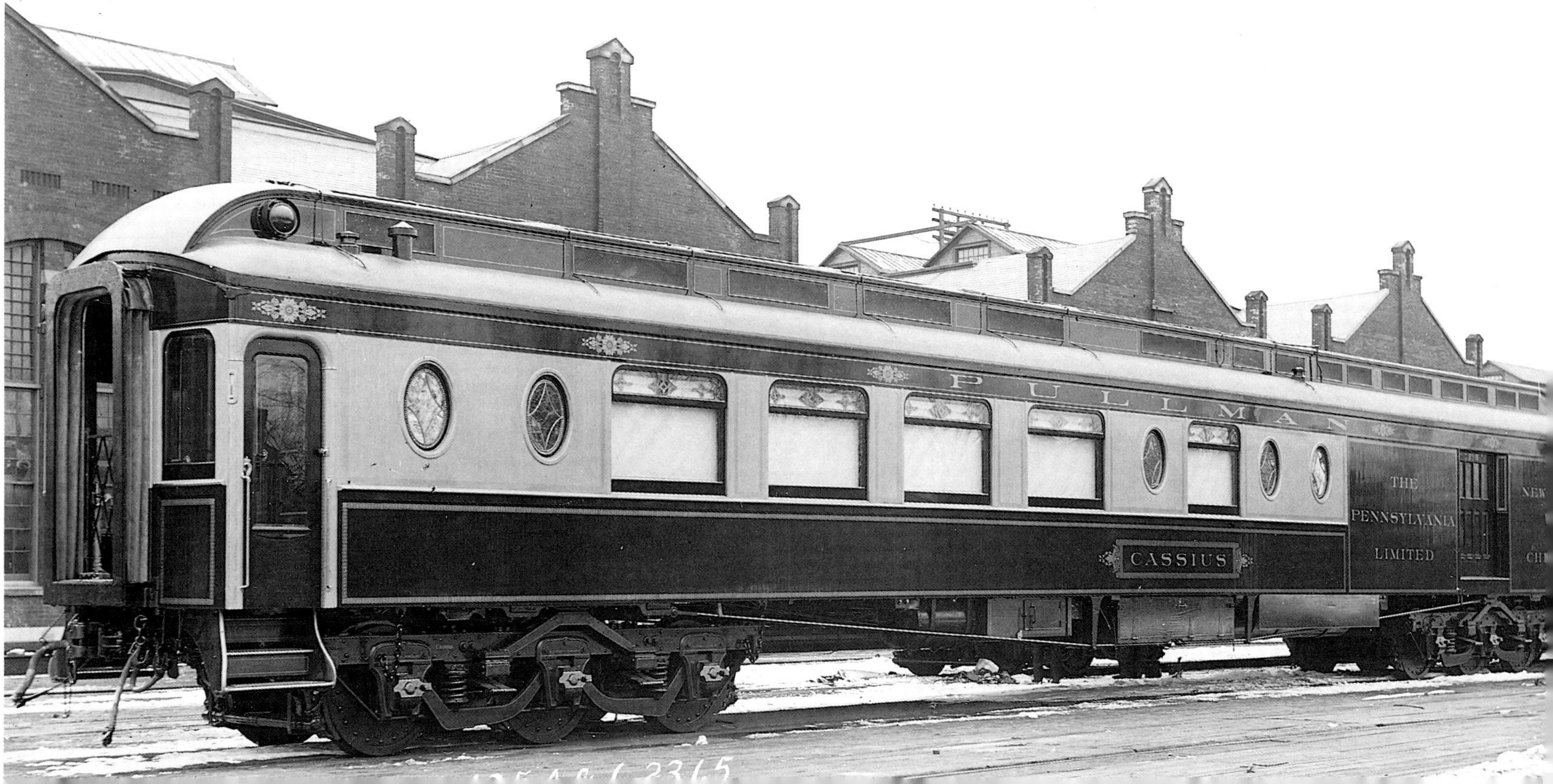

On October 31, 1881, the Pennsylvania Railroad inaugurated a new train between New York and Chicago called the *New York and Chicago Limited*. A detailed description of this train appeared in the *New York Times* of October 29, 1881.

"The Pennsylvania is to make a strong bid for the better class of through business from New York. A reporter of *The Times* learned that by putting on a new, fast train to Chicago, the time will be very much shortened. The trip between the two cities will be made in a little less than 26 hours. The accommodations on this train will be limited. There will be only a certain number of cars allowed, and by this arrangement the chance of detention to the train by adding cars at any point will be overcome....

The Chicago Limited, as this train is to be called, will be composed of parlor, sleeping and dining coaches only, and none but passengers for Harrisburg, Pittsburgh, Fort Wayne, Chicago, and points beyond will be carried. Between New York and Pittsburgh the schedule provides for only three stops. Breakfast will be served immediately after the train leaves Jersey City, dinner after leaving Harrisburg, which will be about 1 o'clock, supper at 6 o'clock in the evening, before reaching Pittsburgh, and breakfast the following morning before the train reaches Chicago. The price of each meal has been placed at 75 cents. All through tickets that are good for first class passage will be honored on this train, but an extra charge will be made for seats in the cars. The rates will be $2 to Harrisburg, $4 to Pittsburgh, $8 to Fort Wayne, and $8 to Chicago.

THE YELLOW KID was the nickname applied to PRR trains 2 and 5, the *Pennsylvania Limited*, in 1898 The monicker was adapted from a popular comic strip character of the day, and referenced the train's creme-yellow window-band livery. *Painting of the Yellow Kid by Larry Fisher, courtesy L. Fisher Prints, Minot, ND*

In speaking of this train yesterday, Mr. Samuel Carpenter, the General Eastern Passenger Agent of the road, said his company was, to a certain extent, forced to put it on the road. The low rates at which Western tickets were selling, he said, had a tendency to attract a very promiscuous class of travel and overcrowd the trains. Objection had been made by the regular patrons, and the new train would afford such of them as desired an opportunity to make the trip in the most speedy and comfortable manner

Reading Company G3 Pacific 213 hustles westbound Jersey Central train 193, the *Harrisburg Special* through Easton, Pennsylvania in September, 1948. This run and its counterpart *Queen of the Valley* were the descendants of the first through New York (Jersey City)- Chicago sleepers, which operated over the CRR of NJ to Allentown, thence the Reading west to a PRR connection in Harrisburg. The through sleeper service became known as the Allentown Route.

Photo/George E. Votava

possible. Mr. Carpenter believed that it would become as popular as the present "limited express" which has been running between New York and Washington for the past six years."

Arthur Dubin, in his book, *Some Classic Trains*, noted June 15, 1887 as the date the Pennsylvania Lines put into service the *Pennsylvania Limited*. At that time the train was composed entirely of Pullman vestibuled cars. Dubin also described *The Pennsylvania Limited* as the predecessor of *The Broadway Limited*.

Douglas Wornom, in his book, *History, Passenger Train and Through Car Service, Pennsylvania Railroad 1849-1947* noted that in October 1891 *The New York and Chicago Limited* was renamed *The Pennsylvania Limited* in the Lines East representation. He noted that Lines West had used this name for some time.

On January 15, 1898 four sets of *Pennsylvania Limited* trains, in an attractive and striking paint scheme, were inaugurated. The cars were built by the Pullman Palace Car Company in Chicago. Each car was Brewster green below the window sash, a cream yellow above, with a red letterboard and decorations in gold. The train was affectionately called "The Yellow Kid" by PRR employees. Each train consisted of a parlor, smoking, and library car, a dining car, three drawing room sleeping cars and an observation car.

A typical consist of this train would include parlor-baggage car *Cassius*, Pullman dining car *Lucullus*, sleeping cars *Cresheim*, *London* and *Logansport*, and observation-compartment car *Fortuna*.

On June 15, 1902 *The Pennsylvania Limited* was replaced by a newer and faster train, the *Pennsylvania Special*. The *Pennsylvania Limited* continued to be listed in the Pennsy passenger timetables long after World War II, even through the Penn Central era up to the creation of Amtrak.

CENTRAL RAILWAY OF NEW JERSEY.
NEW YORK TO EASTON.

John T. Johnson, President. R. E. Ricker, Gen. Superintendent. H. P. Baldwin, Gen. Passenger Agent. P. H. Wyckoff, Gen. Freight Agent.

General Offices of Company—103 Liberty Street, New York City.

CRR of NJ timetable of May 20, 1868 shows connections with the PRR at Harrisburg, with through sleeper to Chicago. The 9:00 A.M. train from New York carried a Pullman Palace Sleeping Car. From *Traveler's Official Guide of the Railways*, June 1868; courtesy National Railway Publication Company.

Sunday Trains—Express train leave New York at 8 p.m., making no stops on the Central Railway of New Jersey. Arrive in New York at 5-10 and 11 50 a.m., making no stops on the Central Railway of New Jersey. All other trains from Easton for New York run daily, Sundays excepted.

PRR K4s 1985 hauls a nine-car *Broadway Limited* through Elizabeth, New Jersey on June 22, 1919. Note turn of the century advertising on billboards at right.
SMITHSONIAN INSTITUTION: Print No. 6326

Form 50

PRR timetable booklet of September 28, 1930 continued the "Broad Way" theme. In addition to listing East-West through schedules, individual pages highlighted the route, schedule and services of many of the individual premier trains, including the *Broadway Limited*.
Tom Gallo Collection

Chapter Two:

Birth and Development of the Broadway Limited

June 15, 1902 was an exciting day for the managements of both the Pennsylvania and New York Central Railroads, for on that day the Pennsy's *Pennsylvania Special* and the Central's *Twentieth Century Limited* were inaugurated. Both trains operated on a twenty hour schedule between New York and Chicago. In 1912, the *Pennsylvania Special* name was changed to *The Broad Way Limited* (later condensed as the *Broadway Limited*). June 15, 1902 marks the beginning of the great rivalry between two great trains, which lasted until the late 1950's.

The excitement of the premier runs of these two deluxe fast trains was captured by the *New York Times* of June 16, 1902:

PENNSYLVANIA'S FAST TRAIN
Pittsburgh, Penn. June 15 - The New York and Chicago specials, the new twenty hour trains on the Pennsylvania Railroad, passed each other on the western outskirts of this Allegheny city. The westbound, No. 29, was on time to the second; the eastbound No. 30 was two minutes late.

Not an incident occurred to mar the passage of the train which left New York, but the sister train, which started from Chicago with every berth occupied but five uppers, had many obstacles to overcome. West of Alliance, on what is known as the Middle Division, No. 30 encountered a runaway freight train.

The passenger crew soon had it under control and the special got behind it and pushed

Rear view of Train 29, the westbound *Broadway Limited* at Elizabeth, New Jersey in 1916. An open-platform observation brings up the markers of the seven car train.   SMITHSONIAN INSTITUTION: Print No. 4406

it two miles to the nearest siding, switched it in, and continued on its way. When nearing Alliance another freight train got in its path, and it had to slow up behind the freight. No. 30 was twenty minutes behind schedule time leaving Alliance. It was two minutes behind time reaching Pittsburgh. The Pullman sleeper *Bryn Mawr*, from St. Louis and Cincinnati, was coupled on No. 30, and the special left Pittsburgh five minutes behind schedule, losing some time because the engine was started before the air man had made connections, slowing after running a hundred yards.

The crews changed at Pittsburgh. The new crew which took No. 29 consisted of L. G. Hawkins, conductor; William Walker, engineer; C. C. Schrock, fireman; and Frank Hunter, baggage master. The crew taking out No. 30 east from Pittsburgh were George Stevenson, conductor; Alexander Thompson, engineer; L. E. Rush, fireman, and S. O. McMinn, baggage master. Engineer Rush said he would make up the five minutes he was late before he reached Johnstown. It took No. 29 five minutes to change engines and baggage here, and No. 30 eight minutes...."

ABOVE: Pullman *Logansport*, built by the Pullman Company in 1904, had a 12-section, 1-Drawing Room interior. Car saw service on the *Pennsylvania Special*. **SMITHSONIAN INSTITUTION: PRINT No. P7440**

RIGHT: Interior view of sleeper *Logansport*. Note that sections were of the open type. **SMITHSONIAN INSTITUTION: Print No. P7441**

Legendary PRR engineer Martin H. Lee had the honor of operating the first westbound and eastbound trips of *The Pennsylvania Special* over the New York Division of the PRR. Lee was given the honor at the request of PRR President Alexander Cassatt. Lee had impressed President Cassatt a few months before, when on short notice, he took a two-car special pulled by locomotive 804, a class D16a locomotive from Broad Street station in Philadelphia to Jersey City in 79 minutes.

ABOVE: *Liberty Cap* was a baggage-club car with twenty lounge seats and a buffet. Car name references a close-fitting cap worn by the Romans, indicative of freedom and liberty. It was used as a symbol on American coins in 1783. Sister cars were *Liberty Bell, Liberty Boys,* and *Liberty Park. Liberty Cap* was built in 1926 and sold to National Railways of Mexico in 1960.
SMITHSONIAN INSTITUTION: Print No. P30461

LEFT: Interior of *Liberty Cap*, baggage-club car assigned to the *Broadway Limited*. SMITHSONIAN INSTITUTION: Print No. P30462

The New York Central did not sit idle while the PRR improved its accommodations and speed on the run from New York to Chicago. During the summer and fall of 1893, the Central operated a twenty-hour train between New York and Chicago called *The Exposition Flyer*. The purpose of the train was to take travelers to the Columbian Exposition in Chicago. The train was withdrawn when the Exposition closed. In November 1897 the Central put on a permanent deluxe New York to Chicago train called *The Lake Shore Limited*. On June 15, 1902 the Central inaugurated its *Twentieth Century Limited*. A *New York Times* reporter gave the following account of the first run of that train.

Rochester, N.Y., June 15- The New York Central *Twentieth Century Limited* train reached Rochester at 10:30 o'clock tonight, just two minutes ahead of scheduled time, having made the run to this city, a distance of 446 miles, in 371 minutes. Along the line there were large crowds of people present to watch the new flier.

The train left New York at exactly 2:45 o'clock. It was composed of the engine, No. 2000, one of the Central Atlantic type, and four cars, each of which was a model of convenience and elegance. The first 100 miles were covered in exactly 119 minutes.

Albany was the first stopping place. That city was reached five minutes ahead of schedule. A change of engines was made, and then the train whisked along to Utica, which was reached two minutes ahead of schedule. A start was made for Syracuse over

ABOVE: DD-1 electrics 3994 and 3995 at Manhattan Transfer circa 1914. PRR trains, including the *Broadway Limited* were hauled through the North River Tunnels into Pennsylvania Station, New York by DD-1's until the AC overhead electrification was completed in the 1930's. Opening of the North River Tunnels in November, 1910 placed the *Broadway Limited* in a better competitive position with New York Central's *Twentieth Century Limited*. SMITHSONIAN INSTITUTION: Print Number 3132.

RIGHT: Two 0-1 electric locomotives haul a nine-car *Broadway Limited* westward from the North River Tunnels in North Bergen, New Jersey on September 25, 1932. SMITHSONIAN INSTITUTION: Print Number 17043.

LIBERTY PARK, a baggage-club car built in 1925 included an onboard barber shop. Car was named for PRR station in Camden County, NJ. *Liberty Park* was sold to Canadian National in 1941 and converted to a coach.
SMITHSONIAN INSTITUTION: Print No. P29581.

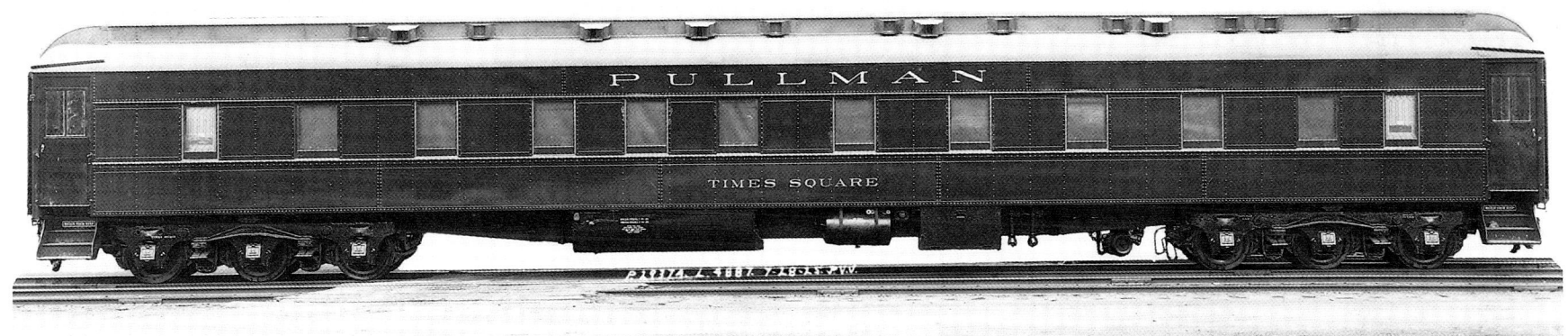

TIMES SQUARE, a 6-compartment, 3-drawing room Pullman built in 1925 and assigned to the *Broadway Limited*. The car eventually went to the Ohio Railway Museum.
SMITHSONIAN INSTITUTION: Print No. P29374.

FEDERAL HALL, a 4-compartment observation lounge built for the *Broadway Limited* in 1925. The car was converted to coach 1190 by the PRR in 1942
SMITHSONIAN INSTITUTION: Print No. P29600.

a stretch of roadbed considered one of the best in the country. The *Empire State Express* covers the distance of 53 miles in 53 minutes, but the *Twentieth Century* covered it in 51 minutes, with Engineer Kendrick W. Bishop at the throttle. This was the fastest time made on the journey.

Syracuse was reached eight minutes ahead of time. Here another change of engines was made, and the trip to Rochester begun. The distance of 81 miles was covered in 89 minutes. The train carried twenty-seven passengers and a large number of New York Central officials and newspaper men, including John W. Gates, the millionaire steel magnate. He was greatly interested in the train and its equipment, and declared that it was the most magnificent train in the world.

The PRR's *Pennsylvania Special* had to be withdrawn on February 1, 1903 due to freight traffic congestion. It was restored on June 11, 1905 and was run on an eighteen-hour schedule between New York and Chicago. The New York Central matched the reduced running time of *The Pennsylvania Special* by reducing the running time of *The Twentieth Century Limited* to 18 hours.

On November 27, 1910 *The Pennsylvania Special* became a more competitive train upon the opening of the North River tunnels and Pennsylvania Station in New York City. Prior to this date, *The Special* required a ferry connection at Exchange Place, Jersey City, for connections to New York.

Concern about safety, particularly in winter, when visibilities were reduced, resulted in the slowing of both *The Century*

BROADWAY LIMITED HEAVYWEIGHT LOUNGE CARS, 1922-1938

by E. Lewis Pardee

When Pullman travel dropped to an all time low on the *Broadway Limited* in 1932, the Pennsylvania Railroad took steps to reduce its losses. With as few as 38 passengers on some trips it was decided to include a Postal car to help defray the cost of operation.

The PRR rebuilt some of its M-70 R.P.O. cars to include a small baggage space (10' x 9 1/4') at one end of each car to handle the checked passenger baggage formerly accommodated in the Pullman Club Baggage car. However, the Club Baggage car also had the barber shop, bath, and served as the forward buffet. These cars were *Liberty Cap, Liberty Colors, Liberty Hill,* and *Liberty Street*.

Pullman withdrew two cars originally built in 1927 as part of a group of 12 similar cars known as Lot 6076, Plan 3975-B, which had been placed in service on two western trains, the *Sunshine Special* and *Texas Special*. The two cars Pullman reassigned to the Pennsylvania were the *Texas City* and *Texas Route* and were renamed *The Broadway* and *Broadway Limited* respectively. A new plan designated as No. 3965-G was assigned to the cars, which had 1 compartment, 1 drawing room, barber shop, bath, writing desk, and a lounge seating 19 people. The cars also had a sunroom solarium, but were always operated in mid-train, usually just ahead of the dining car. Thus, the problem of the barber, bath and forward buffet service was solved, with the addition of a drawing room and a compartment which produced additional revenue. These cars operated in the train until June 15, 1938 when the new lightweight streamlined *Broadway* was inaugurated.

After they were withdrawn from the *Broadway*, they were renamed *Andrew W. Mellon* and *Richard Beatty Mellon* in 1939. Some time in 1940 they replaced the 5 single-bedroom buffet lounge cars on *The Pittsburgher*. This train still carried a baggage club on the head end which continued for some years. There is no indication that the barber and bath facilities were used after reassignment to *The Pittsburgher*; although the Pullman plan was revised June 18, 1942, still showing the barber shop and bath. Seat numbers had been assigned to the lounge chairs. This was probably due to a wartime requirement that such space be available for sale. The final plan was No. 3975-V. These cars served until 1955 when they were scrapped.

I saw both cars often when I watched trains from the platforms of North Philadelphia Station and the passage of the *Broadway* with only five sparsely filled cars on a Saturday night was a sad sight indeed. Happier times for me were riding them on *The Pittsburgher* when the lounges were well patronized by New York and Steel City businessmen relaxing with their nightcaps before retiring. My only regret was that the rear windows of the solarium always faced the end of another car, instead of looking out on the railroad as was their intended purpose.

THE BROADWAY, a 2-compartment, 1-drawing room buffet lounge with sun room, was assigned to the *Broadway Limited*. The car was built in 1927 as the *Texas City* and assigned to the *Texas Special*. It was renamed *The Broadway* in 1933, and again renamed *Richard Beatty Mellon* in 1939. It was withdrawn from service in 1956.
Photo/Robert J. Wayner Collection

and *The Special*. With the lengthening of the schedule for both trains from eighteen to twenty hours, the Pennsylvania announced that its train would now be called *The Broad Way Limited*. The name referred to the PRR's broad right of way over which the train traveled. Some newspapers, however, misunderstood, and right away began spelling it *Broadway Limited*. The New York Times of November 9, 1912 noted the new schedules in an article entitled, *Fast Chicago Trains Are To Run Slower*:

"....During the period of severe winter weather, the *Twentieth Century Limited* on the New York Central will leave New York at 2:45 P.M., arriving in Chicago at 9:45 A.M.; returning it will leave Chicago at 12:40 P.M., and will arrive in this city at 9:40 A.M.

At present the *Twentieth Century Limited* leaves New York at 4 P.M., and reaches Chicago at 8:55 A.M. Upon the return trip it leaves Chicago at 2:30 P.M. and gets in the Grand Central Station at 9:25 A.M.

....The Pennsylvania will on November 24 discontinue its eighteen-hour trains between New York and Chicago, and put into operation a new train to be called the *Broadway Limited*, leaving this city at 2:45 P.M. each day and arriving in Chicago at 9:45 A.M. Eastbound it will leave Chicago at 12:40 P.M. and arrive in New York at 9:40 A.M."

Another reason why *The Pennsylvania Special* was renamed *The Broad Way Limited* by the PRR was confusion by passengers with *The Pennsylvania Limited* which was still in the schedule and had the same route as the *Special*.

RIGHT: PRR Extra Fare Refund Coupon from the *Broadway Limited*, used to secure refund of the extra fare if the *Broadway* was 55 or more minutes late.
Howard B. Morris Collection

BELOW: Illustration from PRR pamphlet timetable dated September 28, 1930.   **Tom Gallo Collection**

On December 1, 1917 *The Broadway Limited* was withdrawn from service upon orders of the United States Railroad Administration due to wartime restrictions. It was restored to service on May 25, 1919.

The Washington section of the *Broadway Limited* was inaugurated on May 6, 1923. This train was an expansion of the Washington sleeping car service consolidated with *The Broadway Limited* at Harrisburg. After little more two years' service, *The Washington Broadway* was discontinued, when on September 27, 1925 the train was renamed *The Liberty Limited*.

The Liberty Limited was well patronized until 1935, when the New York Central's subsidiary, Pittsburgh & Lake Erie granted trackage rights through the Pittsburgh area to the Baltimore & Ohio. Included in the agreement was the use of the Pittsburgh & Lake Erie Railroad through passenger station in Pittsburgh by Baltimore & Ohio passenger trains. Prior to this agreement, B&O passenger trains used their road's Smithfield Street Terminal. Since this was a stub sta-

"When the Broad Way Meets the Dawn"

BROADWAY LIMITED.
No. 29 daily.

Lv. NEW YORK, N. Y.	
Pennsylvania Station (E.S.T.)	3.00 P. M.
Hudson Terminal	2.50 P. M.
Lv. NEWARK, N. J. (Market Street)	3.20 P. M.
Lv. NORTH PHILADELPHIA, PA. (Note A)	4.40 P. M.
Ar. PITTSBURGH, PA.	12.40 A. M.
Ar. ENGLEWOOD, ILL. (C.S.T.)	d9.35 A. M.
Ar. CHICAGO, ILL. (Union Station)	10.00 A. M.

Note A—At North Philadelphia Station there is a station of the North Broad Street Subway in which trains run frequently to and from City Hall Station at Broad and Market Streets. Running time 12 Minutes.

"d" Stops only to discharge passengers.

New York to Chicago 20 hours
Philadelphia to Chicago 18½ hours

Extra fare is charged on this train from New York

To Altoona, Pa.	$3.60	To Fort Wayne, Ind.	$8.40
Chicago, Ill.	9.60	Pittsburgh, Pa.	4.80
Englewood, Ill.	9.60		

Extra fare is charged on this train from North Philadelphia

To Altoona, Pa.	$2.40	To Fort Wayne, Ind.	$7.20
Chicago, Ill.	8.40	Pittsburgh, Pa.	3.60
Englewood, Ill.	8.40		

For extra fares from or to other points, consult ticket agent.

CAR SERVICE.
Club Car.......New York to Chicago.
Sleeping Cars...New York to Chicago—12 Sections Drawing-Room
  New York to Chicago—14 Sections.
  New York to Chicago—13 Single Rooms.
  New York to Chicago—6 Compartments, 3 Drawing-Rooms
Observation Car..New York to Chicago—4 Compartments
Dining Cars.....New York to Altoona.
  Alliance to Chicago.
No Coach Service.

RIGHT: PRR K4 5493 at Chicago on August 20, 1937. Note *Broadway Limited* nameplate beneath PRR Keystone.
Photo/Robert F. Collins.

tion in Pittsburgh by Baltimore & Ohio passenger trains. Prior to this agreement, B&O passenger trains used their road's Smithfield Street Terminal. Since this was a stub station, it involved a tedious and time consuming operation of backing in one direction or the other. The net result of the new arrangement was to shorten the running time of B&O's *Capitol Limited* between Washington and Chicago. With street running through York, PA, and backward running from Washington to Baltimore, *The Liberty Limited* could do little more to speed up its schedule to compete with *The Capitol Limited*. Pennsy's *Liberty Limited* was discontinued in 1957.

In the mid-1920's *The Broadway Limited* and Pennsy New York to St. Louis *American* used all-steel equipment named for distinguished men, women and places prominent in the history of the United States. *The Broadway* had cars assigned with names such as *Liberty Cap*, a baggage-club car with 20 lounge seats and a buffet; *James Logan*, a standard 12-section, 1 drawing-room sleeper, and *Times Square*, which contained 6 compartments, a ladies' lounge, and an open observation platform.

The Pennsylvania Railroad prepared a descriptive booklet explaining the significance of the name assigned to each car.

ABOVE: The Twentieth Century Limited is seen at Fordham Station in the Bronx on June 9, 1938 during the final days of its heavyweight era. The restyled, streamlined Century debuted June 15, 1938. Alco-GE T-3a 282 has a 13-car westbound Train 25 in tow.
UPPER RIGHT: Rear view of the heavyweight Century on June 9, 1938.
RIGHT: TIOGA VALLEY, built in 1930 for NYC's Southwestern Limited had 1 drawing room, 1 single bedroom, buffet and observation-lounge. Car was subsequently assigned to Twentieth Century Limited, seen bringing up Century markers at Harmon, New York on May 30, 1938. Car went to Vermont in August, 1938 and was scrapped in 1958.
                        Three photos/George E. Votava

Publicity efforts of the Pennsylvania Railroad and the New York Central Railroad evolved in subtle ways. The PRR's route from New York to Chicago was shorter than the Central's, but it had to contend with the Allegheny Mountains. The New York Central route was longer but there were no mountains to climb, thus it touted its line as "The Water Level Route" and added "you can sleep." To press this point further, the

The completion of electrification from New York City to Harrisburg, Pennsylvania and the introduction of GG1 electric locomotives significantly reduced the running time of the *Broadway Limited*. PRR GG1 4811 leads an eight-car, westbound *Broadway Limited* through the reverse curve at Elizabeth, New Jersey on May 22, 1937.
Photo/George E. Votava

ABOVE: Illustration from June 25, 1933 PRR system timetable, touting the benefits of its lofty mountain route through the Alleghenies. RIGHT: New York Central countered with emphasis on their smooth, level-running "Water Level Route" as depicted in its September 24, 1939 system schedule.
Joel Rosenbaum Collection

New York Central system timetable maps showed the New York Central route paralleling the Hudson River, and Lakes Ontario, Erie, and Michigan while the on southerly Pennsy route they accentuated the rugged mountains. This suggested that Pennsy Pullman passengers might be thrown out of their beds, as *The Broadway Limited* and other trains twisted up and down mountains and wound through numerous river valleys. The Central refused to identify its 4-8-2 type locomotives as Mountain types, as they were

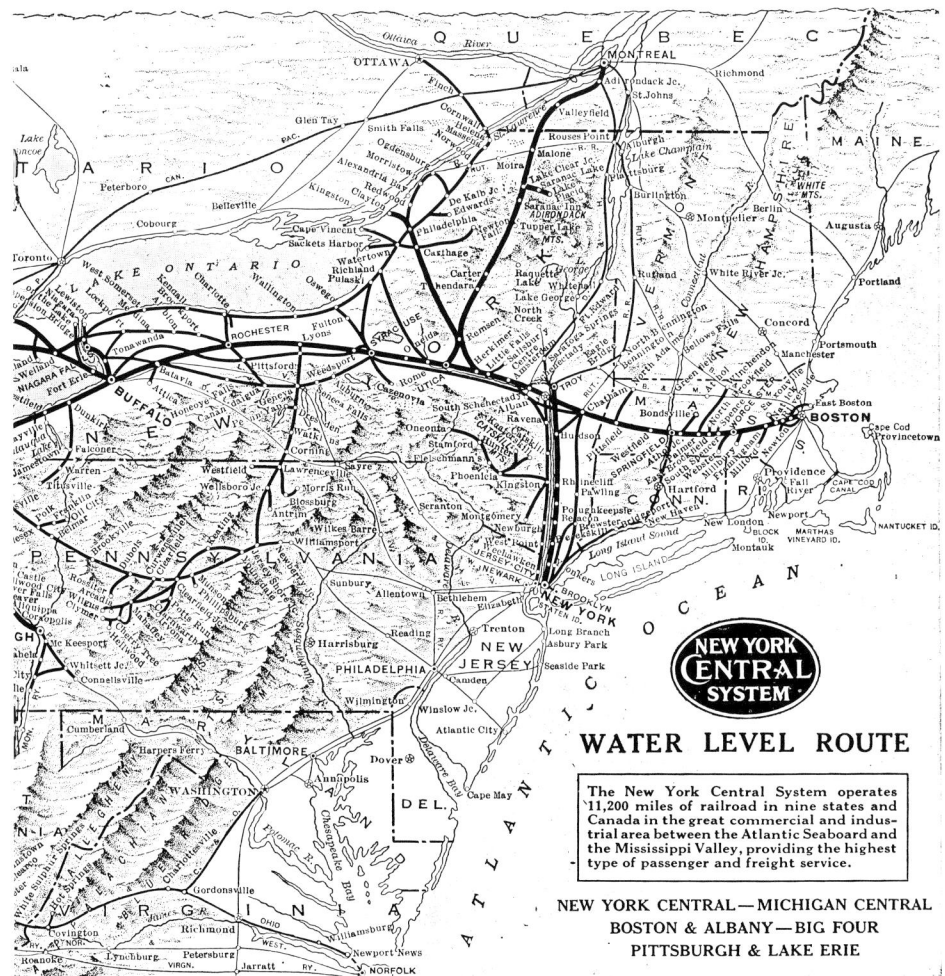

shown in White's classification. Instead, the Central named them Mohawks/ The Pennsy tended to downplay the mountain barriers and failed to show them on their system maps.

Where the Central rolled out a red carpet for *Century* passengers to tread upon, the Pennsy used a different technique to herald the departure of *The Broadway*. A bugler blew a fanfare from the steps of the Savarin Restaurant in Pennsylvania Station. He then would march through the concourse, and sound the bugle at the train gate. Redcaps would all leap to attention and chorus, *...Broadway Limited leaving at 5:00 P.M. from Track Twelve!*

Consistently *The Century* carried more passengers than *The Broadway* and often ran in several sections. During the depth of the Depression *The Broadway* operated with only five or six cars on Saturday nights.

Through its career as an all-Pullman train, *The Pennsylvania Special* and *The Broadway Limited* were assigned numbers 28 and 29.

CONDENSED SCHEDULE OF TRAINS EASTWARD

The time from 12.01 A.M. to 12 o'clock noon, inclusive, is indicated by light-face type; from 12.01 P.M. to 12 o'clock midnight, inclusive, by heavy face type.	The Red Arrow 68	The Golden Arrow 78	"Spirit of St. Louis" 30	The Rainbow 42	Seaboard Exp. 34	Keystone Exp. 20-34	The Pennsylvania Limited 2	Commercial Exp. 26	Eastern Exp. 8	The Gotham Limited 54	The Juniata 44
	Daily ⊕ P M	Daily ⊕ P M	Daily ⊕ P M	Daily P M	Daily A M	Daily A M	Daily ⊕ P M	Daily ⊕ P M	Daily P M	Daily ⊕ P M	Daily ●8.00
Lv. Chicago, Ill. (Via Ft.Wayne) (C.S.T.)		2.00		4.00			6.00		3.00	9.00	●8.00
Lv. Chicago, Ill. (Via Columbus)	No Coaches Detroit to New York	2.17		4.17	10.45 11.02		6.17		3.19	9.17 6.00 7.40	9.17 4.50
Lv. Englewood, Ill.			12.02 1.30 4.55 1.15 6.10 9.55			9.10 3.20 1.15 6.10	12.10 1.30 7.05		No Coaches Chicago to New York	11.00 5.05 10.50 4.15 11.15	10.00 3.50 11.15
Lv. St. Louis, Mo.											
Lv. Louisville, Ky.											
Lv. Indianapolis, Ind.											
Lv. Louisville, Ky. (L. & N.)											
Lv. Cincinnati, O. (E.S.T.)											
Lv. Columbus, O.					8.40	10.05		1.50			
Lv. Detroit, Mich	4.15			7.50							
Lv. Toledo, O.	5.38		No Coaches	9.15						1.05	1.05
Lv. Cleveland, O.	8.20							12.50			
Lv. Pittsburgh, Pa.	12.04	1.03	2.28	3.50	3.53	3.53	6.05	7.10	8.00	9.10	9.25
Ar. West Philadelphia, Pa. (32nd and Market Sts.)									5.50		
Ar. Philadelphia, Pa., Broad St. Sta. (Broad and Market Sts.)									5.55		
Ar. North Philadelphia, Pa.	d 7.49	d 9.04	10.19	12.04	1.23	1.23	2.02	3.35	6.23	d5.02	5.21
Ar. Newark, N.J.	9.08	10.30	11.40	1.26	3.11	3.11	d 3.26	4.58	7.58	6.26	6.48
Ar. New York, N.Y. (Hud. Term.)	9.35	11.00	12.11	1.50	3.39	3.39	3.54	5.25	8.21	6.54	7.11
Ar. New York, N.Y. (Penna. Sta.)	9.30	11.00	12.02	1.50	3.35	3.35	3.50	5.20	8.20	6.50	7.10
	A M	A M	P M	P M	P M	P M	P M	P M	P M	P M	P M

"d" Stops only to discharge passengers.
See pages 32 and 33 for extra fares charged on this train.
⊕ See pages 32 and 33 for extra fares charged on this train.
● Train No. 44 will not be held at Pittsburgh if train from the West is late.

(Continued on next page.)

CONDENSED SCHEDULE OF TRAINS EASTWARD—Continued.

The time from 12.01 A.M. to 12 o'clock noon, inclusive, is indicated by light-face type; from 12.01 P.M. to 12 o'clock midnight, inclusive, by heavy face type.	Day Exp. 124-24	The Duquesne 74	New Englander 46	Steel City Exp. 124-6	Mercantile Exp. 6	The New Yorker 52	Iron City Exp. 16	Buckeye Lim. 38	Manhattan Lim. 22	Broadway Lim. 28	Phila. Night Exp. 36	The American 66	Cincinnati Lim. 40
	Daily P M	Daily P M	Daily P M	Daily P M	Daily A M	Daily P M	Daily P M	Daily ⊕ P M	Daily ⊕ A M	Daily ⊕ N'ON	Daily P M	Daily ⊕ A M	Daily ⊕ A M
Lv. Chicago, Ill. (Via Ft.Wayne) (C.S.T.)	11.45			11.45		10.00				11.17			
Lv. Chicago, Ill. (Via Columbus)		●10.30	10.30			10.17				12.17			
Lv. Englewood, Ill.	12.02	●10.47	10.47	12.02 12.03									No Coaches
Lv. St. Louis, Mo.					7.50 2.30 9.25							9.02	
Lv. Louisville, Ky.												1.50	
Lv. Indianapolis, Ind.							7.25					No Coaches	11.25
Lv. Louisville, Ky. (L. & N.)		●8.00	8.00		1.55		1.10						4.20
Lv. Cincinnati, O. (E.S.T.)							4.10					6.52	7.10
Lv. Columbus, O.							1.30						
Lv. Detroit, Mich							2.57						
Lv. Toledo, O.									7.00				
Lv. Cleveland, O.	8.00	●10.30	10.30	●2.40		●4.25	6.05						
Lv. Pittsburgh, Pa.	11.30	2.15	3.40	7.25	7.25	9.20	●9.30	9.44	10.15	11.05	11.35		11.50
Ar. West Philadelphia, Pa. (32nd and Market Sts.)	8.35	9.55							7.45				
Ar. Philadelphia, Pa., Broad St. Sta. (Broad and Market Sts.)	8.40	10.00							7.50				
Ar. North Philadelphia, Pa.			12.01	4.29	4.29	5.00	d5.50	d5.59	d6.54			d7.16	d7.34
Ar. Newark, N.J.			r 1.28	6.10	6.10	6.41	7.15	7.22	△7.44	8.27		△8.51	9.15
Ar. New York, N.Y. (Hud. Term.)			1.50	6.40	6.40	7.00	7.40	7.55	8.00	9.00		9.04	9.27
Ar. New York, N.Y. (Penna. Sta.)			1.50	6.35	6.35	7.00	7.40	7.55	8.00	9.00		9.02	9.25
	P M	P M	A M	A M	A M	A M	A M	A M	A M	A M		A M	A M

△ Connection arrives Park Place; passengers change at Manhattan Transfer.   ⊕ See pages 32 and 33 for extra fares charged on this train.
† Week-days only.   ● Trains No. 6, 16 and 74 will not be held for connection at Pittsburgh if trains from the West are late.
"d" Stops only to discharge passengers.   "r" Stops only on notice to Conductor to discharge passengers from points west of Philadelphia.

Railroad Fares and Pullman Sleeping Car Fares, including Railroad surcharge.

Subject to Change.

Pullman Fares Quoted Include Railroad Surcharge.

NEW YORK TO	Railroad Fare.	Upper Berth.	Lower Berth.	Compartment.	Drawing Room.
Akron, O.	$20.08	$4.50	$5.63	$15.75	$21.00
Alliance, O.	18.81	4.50	5.63	15.75	21.00
Chicago, Ill.	32.70	7.20	9.00	25.50	31.50
Cincinnati, O.	27.01	6.00	7.50	21.00	27.00
Cleveland, O.	20.55	4.50	5.63	15.75	21.00
Columbus, O.	22.70	5.10	6.38	18.00	22.50
Coshocton, O.	20.24	4.50	5.63	15.75	21.00
Crestline, O.	22.63	5.10	6.38	18.00	22.50
Dayton, O.	25.24	6.00	7.50	21.00	27.00
Detroit, Mich.	24.82	5.10	6.38	18.00	22.50
Effingham, Ill.	34.23	7.80	9.75	27.75	34.50
Elwood, Ind.	28.48	6.60	8.25	23.25	30.00
Ft. Wayne, Ind.	26.20	6.00	7.50	21.00	27.00
Gary, Ind.	31.70	7.20	9.00	25.50	31.50
Indianapolis, Ind.	29.20	7.20	9.00	25.50	31.50
Kokomo, Ind.	29.20	6.60	8.25	23.25	30.00
Lima, O.	25.22	6.00	7.50	21.00	27.00
Logansport, Ind.	29.83	6.60	8.25	23.25	30.00
Louisville, Ky.	31.32	7.20	9.00	25.50	31.50
Mansfield, O.	22.14	5.10	6.38	18.00	22.50
Memphis, Tenn.	41.71	10.20	12.75	36.00	45.00
Nashville, Tenn.	34.75	8.10	10.13	28.50	36.00
Newark, O.	21.51	5.10	6.38	18.00	22.50
New Castle, Ind.	27.72	6.60	8.25	23.25	30.00
Niles, O.	18.49	3.60	4.50	12.75	16.50
Piqua, O.	25.33	6.00	7.50	21.00	27.00
Pittsburgh, Pa.	15.82	3.60	4.50	12.75	16.50
Port Columbus, O.	22.45	5.10	6.38	18.00	22.50
Richmond, Ind.	26.74	6.60	8.25	23.25	30.00
St. Louis, Mo.	38.06	8.70	10.88	30.75	39.00
Springfield, O.	24.68	See Pullman Fares to Xenia.			
Steubenville, O.	17.38	3.60	4.50	12.75	16.50
Terre Haute, Ind.	31.78	7.20	9.00	25.50	31.50
Toledo, O.	24.40	5.10	6.38	18.00	22.50
Urbana, O.	24.39	5.10	6.38	18.00	22.50
Valparaiso, Ind.	31.12	6.60	8.25	23.25	30.00
Wheeling, W. Va.	18.20	4.50	5.63	15.75	21.00
Warsaw, Ind.	28.78	6.60	8.25	23.25	30.00
Xenia, O.	24.68	6.00	7.50	21.00	27.00
Youngstown, O.	18.16	3.60	4.50	12.75	16.50

A minimum of two (2) adult first-class passage tickets (or their equivalent) will be required for the exclusive occupancy of a compartment or drawing-room in sleeping cars.

A minimum of one (1) adult ticket is required for the exclusive occupancy of a section in sleeping car.

K-4 3768 received complete streamlining. Note *Broadway Limited* nameplate on smokebox and PRR keystone with wings. This locomotive was difficult to service due to its shrouding, and was not strictly used in *Broadway Limited* service. No. 3768 is seen at Englewood, Illinois in 1938.
Bob Lorenz Collection

 Chapter Three:

A Fleet of Modernism-- The 1938 Streamlined Broadway Limited

On June 15, 1938 both the Pennsylvania and New York Central Railroads inaugurated completely re-equipped, streamlined *Broadway Limited* and *Twentieth Century* consists. The *Twentieth Century Limited* was supported with four new trains sets. The Pennsylvania re-equipped only two complete trainsets for *The Broadway*, while six other new sets were assigned to the *General* (NY-Chicago), the *Liberty Limited* (Washington-Chicago), and the *Spirit of St. Louis* (NY-St. Louis).

On the new *Broadway*, five types of private room accommodations were provided. These were the master bedroom, the drawing room, compartment, double bedroom, and the roomette. With the inauguration of the new streamlined train, section sleepers were no longer assigned to *The Broadway*.

The streamlined *Broadway* had a specially arranged lounge car and a distinctive diner midway in the train. A new type of observation car brought up the rear of the train. The observation car had outward facing sofas and club chairs from which passengers could enjoy the passing scenery. Both the lounge and observation cars were equipped with refreshment sections.

The dining cars for the streamlined *Broadway* were rebuilt and refinished by the Pennsylvania Railroad shops at Altoona, PA. The 1938 streamlined *Broadway Limited*-- from its locomotives to its cars was styled by noted industrial designer Raymond Loewy. The diners featured arch roofs and dining areas which were separated by a center lounge section. In each of the dining rooms were two double tables on one side of the aisle, with two single tables on the other. In front of each of the middle lounge seats was a pedestal type table which accommodated two people. At the steward's end of the car were a tavern nook and a service bar. Seating capacity was 30.

The narrow bulkheads which separated the dining rooms from the central lounge were finished in lace Flexwood which was light tan in tone. The window posts were fitted with mirrors and the frieze above the windows was decorated with a gold mottled paper. The side ceilings were cafe au lait, with the mottled gold paper repeated in the center between the air-distribution ducts. The floor was covered with a two-tone burgundy carpet, in salt and pepper pattern, and window drapes were in a lighter tone of the same color. The ceiling trim was in burgundy, gold and blue, while the tables were in gold and the gold chairs were upholstered in light blue leather. Table linen was light tan.

In the center lounge section the side walls were covered with beige finished square tiles of furniture steel, separated with 1/4" strips of polished brass, with a gold star at the center of alternate squares. The bulkheads were lacewood and the ceiling pastel blue, while the lounge seats were upholstered in yellow leather.

STREAMLINED BEAUTY: The T1 multi-cylindered steam passenger locomotive is another masterpiece created from the 100 years of experience and research of the Pennsylvania Railroad. T1's could be found on the head end of the *Broadway Limited*, notably on the west end of the railroad.
E.L. Pardee Collection

In the tavern nook the side wall and front of the bar were finished in bubinga Flexwood, brown in tone, with the side ceiling in lemon yellow and burgundy in the center between the ducts. Opposite the bar which had a micarta top, was a yellow leather seat with two stationary pedestal tables. Above the settee were four colorful prints of early Pennsylvania locomotives. The center section of the upper bar had a large rose colored mir-

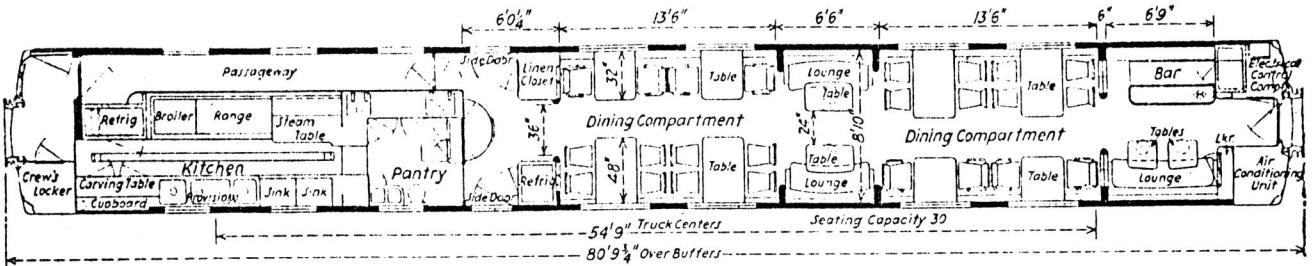

The Dining Cars for the Broadway Limited

ror, with glass shelves between the cupboards which held the glassware.

The bulkhead at the kitchen end of the dining car had an upper section with eight rose colored mirror panels on each side of the aisle. Separating the tavern nook from the dining room was a similar bulkhead with clear glass panels. From floor to ceiling at the pantry passageway was a half-round buffet, the lower section of which was a silver storage cabinet and the upper section featured a rose colored mirror. On the micarta top of the buffet was a permanent flower vase.

The passageway by the kitchen was strikingly decorated with light blue walls, golden ivory ceiling and window drapes in old gold. The rubber floor covering was burgundy relieved with an inlaid pattern in light blue and white.

The lighting was accomplished by a combination of semi-indirect trough fixtures and lens units in the ceiling. In the dining rooms the trough lighting was installed along each side above the windows and was supplemented by a single row of lens units in the center of the ceiling. The lounge and tavern sections were lighted by lens units set in an oval pattern in the ceiling. The passageways were also lighted by the lens type of ceiling unit.

Music was furnished for the passengers and the diner was connected by telephone to other cars in the train.

DINING CARS OF THE BROADWAY LIMITED

by E. L. Pardee

The first *Broadway Limited* dining cars were all-steel class D-70 series cars seating 30 people. These cars were subsequently modified with the addition of six-wheel roller bearing trucks in 1930, and with air conditioning in 1931.

Two D-70's were extensively modified for the new *Broadway* of 1938, but a year later these were replaced by new lightweight class D-78 diners built by Budd, Pullman and ACF. These traditional single-unit lightweight cars served until the introduction of new "twin-unit" sets in 1946. The twin-units were comprised of a kitchen-dormitory car, and an attached full dining room car, which seated 68 passengers.

After a slow start in 1938, the new streamlined *Broadway* saw increased patronage as the war approached. During the war years, business was at capacity, and two single unit diners were run in most *Broadway* consists. This prompted the decision to develop the twin-unit concept.

Dining on the *Broadway* was always something special, for no other train on the PRR system was as respected, nor received the loving care that it did. All *Broadway Limited* onboard personnel began each trip with a boutonniere. Uniforms were inspected by Passenger Department representatives on a regular basis, as was the entire train. Passing through the dining car, all crew members removed their hats in respect to the importance of clients who rode this famous train.

Everyone has a favorite menu item, often depending on locale or railroad. When this writer rode the *Broadway Limited,* one of the two center-of-car tables opposite the bar was sought. These tables seated two passengers, and somehow the service there always appeared to be most impressive. Unique among rolling restaurants was a "hot table" where infrared lamps kept food and plates hot while awaiting delivery to diners' tables.

Both the steaks and the prime rib were exceptionally good, brought to the table on piping hot steel serving plates, to be transferred to china at tableside by a skilled waiter. One could hear the juices sizzling on the hot steel plate as the waiter approached. My favorite was the prime rib of beef: The *Broadway* chefs removed the bone before serving, a practice which I had never observed on any other railroad dining cars.

As would be expected, all *Broadway* meal portions were generous, and worthy of contemplation while sipping a cocktail in the train's rear observation lounge.

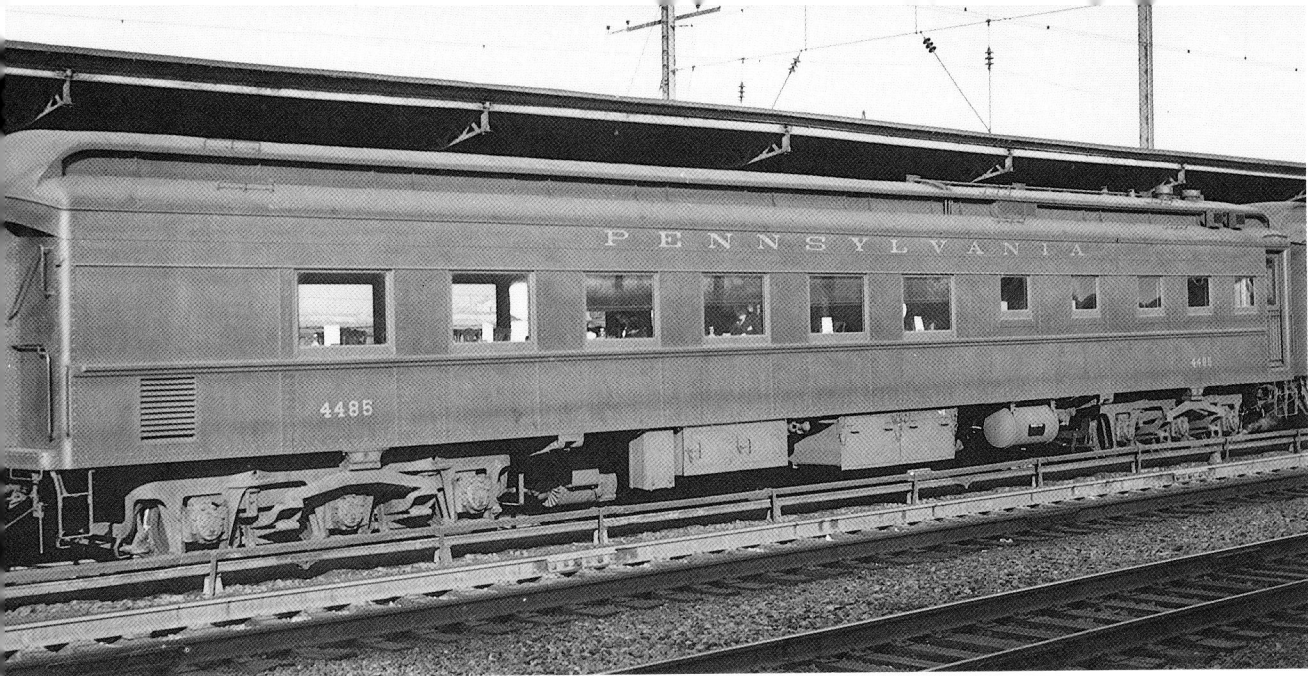

The lounge car for the streamlined *Broadway* had lounge and bar sections, a train secretary's office, barber shop, and two double bedrooms. The lounge contained three sections. In the first was a quarter-circle bar, mirrored to give a complete circular effect. The bar front was redwood burl, combined with brown opalescent finish and figured ribbon mahogany. Two circular settees and two chairs were upholstered in golden mohair, the ceiling was a rose-rust tint, and the Venetian blinds were cedar tan.

The second section was arranged for card players. Figures of face cards were shown in lighted molded glass panels behind the rust mohair seats. The walls were covered in steerhide and the ceilings were copper lacquer.

The lounge proper occupied the third section, which was carpeted in deep mahogany; the movable chairs were in gray-green leather, and the settees were covered in gray mohair. The color note was carried out with dark gray hairwood wainscoting and elephant gray side ceilings.

THE OLD... PRR standard dining car 4485 is seen at Manhattan Transfer, NJ on January 5, 1937. Two similar standard diners, numbers 4420 and 4423 were rebuilt extensively in 1938 for the restyled 1938 *Broadway Limited*.

...AND THE NEW: PRR diner 4515 was built new by Pullman Standard in 1939 for the restyled *Broadway*. The car is seen at Flushing, NY on October 29, 1939 in a livery of two-tone Tuscan and dark maroon. The PRR was at one time the largest operator of dining car service in the United States.   **Two photos/George E. Votava**

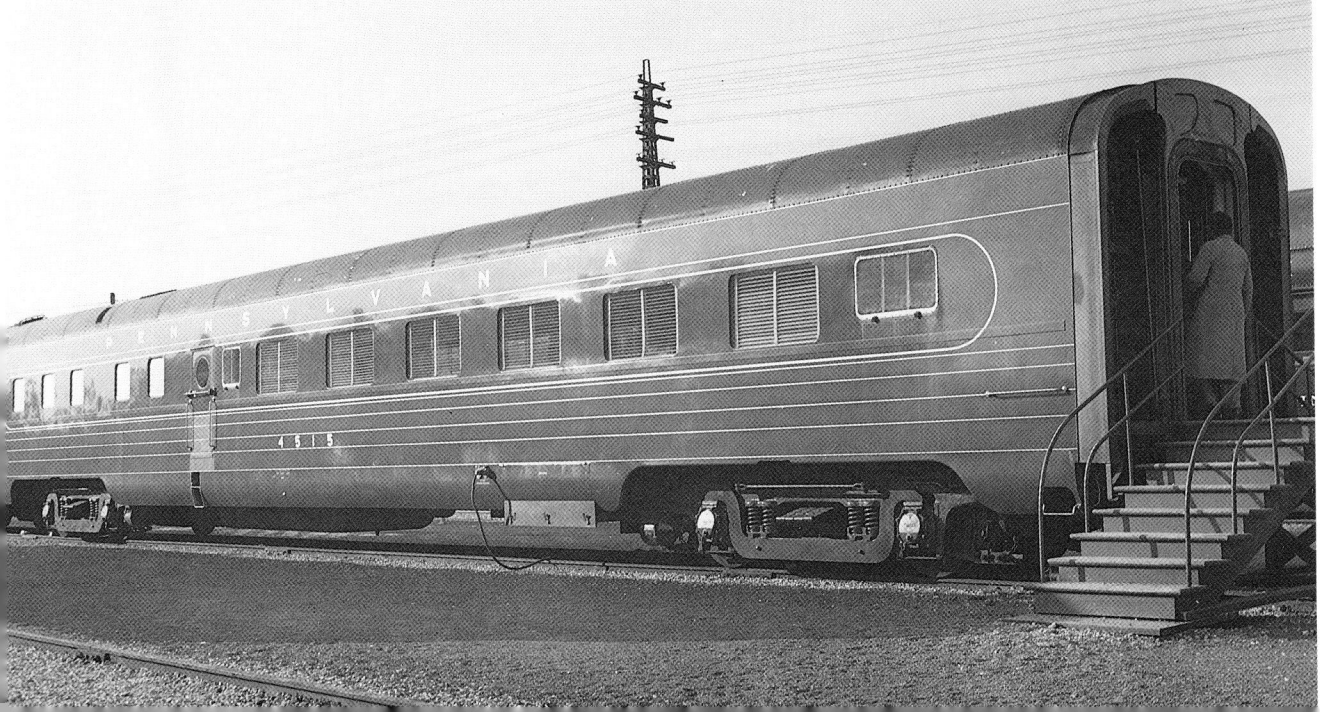

A large Chicago historical mural covered about one-third of the wall space. In the lower half of this mural was a modern conception of the new streamlined *Broadway Limited* in action. The office of the secretary had gray walls, a dusty pink ceiling, tan chairs, and dark cedar carpeting. In addition to providing secretarial services for passengers, the secretary also directed the train's radio and public address system from this office.

In addition to the lounge sections, the *Broadway* observation car had two master bedrooms and a double bedroom. Rounded

BROADWAY LIMITED LIGHTWEIGHT MID-TRAIN LOUNGE CARS
by E. L. Pardee

When the *Broadway Limited* was streamlined in 1938, the barber shop, bath and train secretary's office were reaccommodated in mid-train lounges *Harbor Springs* and *Harbor Point*. These luxurious cars contained a stand-up quarter-circle bar and seated 19 passengers in a semi-divided lounge, with tables for beverages. The cars included revenue space in the form of two double bedrooms located in the middle of the car. These two lounges operated until they were replaced with new cars ordered in 1946. When *Harbor Springs* and *Harbor Point* were replaced on the *Broadway,* the barber shop and bath facilities were discontinued as a feature of the train.

Before the cars were reassigned, they were reconfigured to include five double bedrooms, utilizing space previously occupied by the barber shop, bath and train secretary's office. Bar and lounge space remained unchanged. The cars saw service for many years and became part of PRR's ex-Pullman fleet, at which time they received numbers 8118 and 8119 respectively. For a short time they operated in "day service" between Washington and New York, and the bedrooms were sold at Parlor Car "day room" rates. Traveling from Philadelphia to New York this writer once had the occasion to occupy one of the rooms and changed to dinner attire enroute to a meeting in New York.

LEFT: Mid-train lounge *Harbor Point*, a 2 bedroom-bar-lounge which featured a bath, barber shop and train secretary's office, built for *Broadway Limited* service.
E.L. Pardee Collection

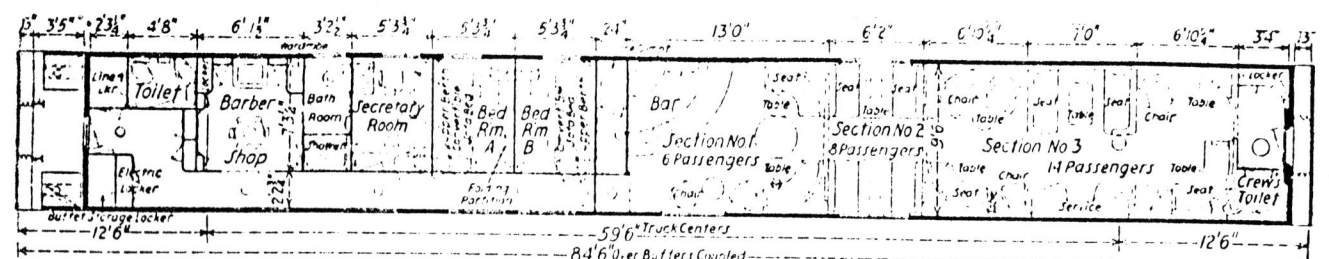

The Lounge Car for the Broadway Limited

ends gave an oval effect to the lounge. A ceiling of copper lacquer followed this contour and contained elaborate indirect lighting. Blue was the predominant color used in the large lounge chairs, the Formica-topped tables at each end, and in the carpets and drapes. The wainscoting was dark blue, with rose tan opalescent lacquer walls and cedar tan Venetian blinds. There were two sections for cards in the center of the lounge with blue leather sofa seats, which contrasted with the gold fabric of the window panels.

The mid-train lounge section of the 1938 *Broadway Limited* featured an historical mural with a modern depiction of the streamlined *Broadway* passing through the North River Tunnels beneath the Hudson River.

Photo/Robert J. Wayner Collection

The Budd Company delivered dining car 4504 to the PRR in August, 1939. The car is seen on display at the New York Worlds Fair in Flushing on September 17, 1939. Budd reportedly was quite unhappy with the PRR covering over its gleaming stainless steel fluted cars with Tuscan red and dark maroon paint.

Photo/George E. Votava

Metropolitan View **was assigned to the original 1938 streamlined** *Broadway Limited,* **along with sister car** *Skyline View***. The rounded-end observation marked a radical change from open platforms.** *Metropolitan View* **was built by Pullman Standard in May, 1938 and is seen at Long Island City, NY on May 2, 1948.**
Photo/George E. Votava

The seating arrangement of the observation car was considered novel. In the front were two rounded sofas with tables, while at the extreme end was a sofa that afforded three different views, one to each side and one to the rear. The corner sofas were in chocolate brown leather and the center sofa was in two-tone taupe. The wainscoting was quartered walnut with walls of natural finish cork and ceiling of light cream.

Pullman *Allegheny County* **was assigned to the 1938** *Broadway Limited.* **Built by Pullman Standard in April 1938,** it was still in its original 1938 scheme of Tuscan red and dark maroon when photographed in Long Island City, NY on May 2, 1948. Photo/George E. Votava

Specific cars assigned to the 1938 streamlined *Broadway Limited* included the following:

18 Roomettes
Plan 4068D, Lot 6539
Pullman-Standard, March 1938
8041 *City of Baltimore*
8044 *City of Cincinnati*
8045 *City of Columbus*
8056 *City of New York*
8058 *City of Philadelphia*
8059 *City of Pittsburgh*
8061 *City of St. Louis*
8064 *City of Washington*

2 Double Bedrooms,
Secretary's Room, Barber Shop,
Shower Bath, Bar-Lounge
Plan 4077, Lot 6550
Pullman-Standard, May 1938
8118 *Harbor Point*
8119 *Harbor Springs*

2 Master Rooms, 1 Double Bedroom,
Buffet Lounge Observation
Plan 4080, Lot 6548
Pullman-Standard, May 1938
8115 *Metropolitan View*
8116 *Skyline View*

4 Compartments, 2 Drawing Rooms,
4 Double Bedrooms
Plan 4069B, Lot 6540
Pullman-Standard, March 1938
8011 *Imperial Park*
8012 *Imperial Pass*
8014 *Imperial Plateau*
8015 *Imperial Point*

13 Double Bedrooms
Plan 4071A, Lot 6541
Pullman-Standard, April 1938
8000 *Allegheny County*
8006 *New York County*

The dining car in each consist was a 4400-series heavyweight diner rebuilt by PRR's Altoona shops.

The exterior paint scheme of the cars featured a dark maroon window band with the rest of the car painted in Tuscan red with gold striping and black roofs.

GG-1 electrics hauled the train between New York and Harrisburg while K-4 Pacific steam locomotives handled the train between Harrisburg and Chicago. Several K-4 locos were streamlined for service on the new train. Included in the streamlining program were K-4 3768 which received complete streamlining, and K-4 1120 which carried a modified streamlined appearance. The PRR was not meticulous in assigning streamlined steam to *The Broadway* and often standard K-4 locos carried the train name on the smokebox just below the headlight.

On June 8, 1938, a week before being placed into regular service on the PRR, a preview run was made between New York and Philadelphia. A flat $2.50 was charged for the round trip. Nine different types of streamlined cars were carried on the 13-car train and a total of 300 passengers were accommodated. The train left Pennsylvania Station at 1:45 P.M., arriving in Philadelphia at 3:15 P.M. The return trip left Philadelphia at 4:00 P.M., making a short stop at Adams, NJ, where it discharged news photographers for a photo runby. The publicity train returned to New York at 8:45 P.M.

ABOVE: K4 1120 acquired partial streamlining for *Broadway Limited* service; seen at Englewood, Illinois in 1941.

BELOW: K5 5699 is seen at Harrisburg station in 1940 waiting to take over the *Broadway* from a GG1 electric.
Two photos/Bob Lorenz collection

ABOVE: Handsome J-3a Hudson 5452 was built by ALCO in April, 1938 for service on the *Twentieth Century Limited;* seen at Harmon, NY on May 30, 1938.
BELOW: Pullman-Standrad delivered 4 double bedroom-buffet-lounge-observation car *Manhattan Island* to the New York Central in 1938 for service of the *Twentieth Century Limited.* Car featured a speedometer and a scale model of a streamlined Hudson locomotive. View is after rebuilding in 1946.

Two photos/George E. Votava

The streamlined *Twentieth Century Limited* of 1938 differed in some respects from *The Broadway*. The New York Central assigned 10 new streamlined J-3a class 4-6-4 Hudson steam locos to service on *The Century*. A model of the streamlined Hudson class of locomotive was placed in a recessed glass-front case in two of the *Century* observation cars. These cars also contained speedometers so the passengers could observe the speed of the train. In the lounge cars were small models of the DeWitt Clinton train and locomotive 999. A distinctive feature of the *Century* diners was following dinner they were transformed into cafes or lounges. Their regular bright lights were turned off and an auxiliary system of lights turned on, illuminating the diner with a soft rose light. Special rust-colored table linen was used during this period, and a phonograph and radio provided popular music of the day. It was noted that although the illumination was subdued, it was sufficient for card playing if this was desired.

The 1938 streamlined *Twentieth Century Limited* was designed through the combined efforts of the New York industrial designer Henry Dreyfuss, and the New York Central's engineering department. The exterior color scheme was light gray with the window area painted dark gray, edged in blue, and set off with two silver stripes. The interior was rust, blue, tan, and gray, using woods, metals, and leathers.

The launching of both The *Broadway* and the *Century* on the thirty-sixth anniversary of their inaugural runs was a real media event to the delight of both railroads.

A *New York Times* editorial *Trains of Splendor* concluded that "all the 'overstuffed' feeling of the old railway car is gone. Everywhere, is a sense of restful living."

The first runs attracted large crowds along the respective rights of way. As the *Century* sped west through the Mohawk Valley in the gathering darkness, there was no let-up in the interest of those wanting to see the gray and blue limited flash by.

The *Broadway's* run, began on its thirty-sixth anniversary, was a sixteen hour celebration. Every passenger and freight engine, railroad yard and factory along the right of way blew whistles as the flier flashed past. In celebration of this event, the *Broadway's* chef baked a huge thirty-sixth anniversary cake for the passengers.

The competition between the Central's *Twentieth Century* and the Pennsy's *Broadway* was by no means just limited to the high iron. The limiteds also competed in the cinema and around the Christmas tree.

In the early thirties there was a successful Broadway play *20th Century* by Ben Hecht and Charles MacArthur. The entire play took place on a simulated *Twentieth Century Limited*. The play was made into a movie starring John Barrymore and Carole Lombard in 1934. The play was revived on Broadway over a decade after the *Twentieth Century* was removed from the timetable. It was again a success. Walter Kerr in reviewing the revival in the November 21, 1978 edition of the *New York Times* noted that "Robin Wagner's remarkable silver trains in *On the Twentieth Century* clap together like a deck of playing cards, giving themselves a fast reshuffle, and then fan out like a 52-card spray held tight against a magician's palm. It's no secret that the musical's restless, glistening undeniably spectacular scenery has been one of the reasons--maybe the major reason for the show's success." Amtrak even offered tickets, the original cast album at reduced prices, and special brochures for the Broadway play.

In 1941, the movie *Broadway Limited*, produced by Hal Roach and released through United Artists made its appearance. For the making of the movie a special car was attached to the real *Broadway Limited* to obtain authentic shots of passengers and to record movie camera views of the familiar sights along the route as passengers would see them. The reviews of the movie were terrible. One *Times* reviewer noted that:

The best, and the worst, that one can say concerning *Broadway Limited*, now at the Globe, is that its producers have quite obviously heard of *Twentieth Century*, the John Barrymore-Carole Lombard lark which was rolling folks in the aisles a few years back. The only difference, and it is a difference, lies in the fact that the *Twentieth Century* started down the tracks with a full head of steam and *Broadway Limited* starts off without a thimbleful.

The highest speed ever reached by *The Broadway Limited* occurred in June, 1905 on the reappearance of *The Pennsylvania special* on an 18-hour schedule. On the maiden westbound trip engineer Jerry McCarthy hit 127 miles per hour near Elida, Ohio to make up for a 25-minute delay caused by a hotbox. E2 Atlantic 7002 did the honors.

Chapter Four:

The Post-War Years

FEBRUARY 9, 1946...a time of transition. A doubleheaded *Broadway Limited* powered by K4 steam locomotives races a diesel powered *Twentieth Century Limited* at Englewood, Illinois.

Photo/Charles A. Brown

It is always a "beautiful day" in Chicago when you arrive well rested after a comfortable trip on the BROADWAY LIMITED.

PENNSYLVANIA RAILROAD

**ABOVE: "Weather Report" for Chicago was issued as a courtesy to *Broadway Limited* passengers...another personal touch aboard the Pennsy's flagship train.
Collection of Joel Rosenbaum**

**Diesels such as E8A 5884 gradually replaced steam after World War II on the Pennsy's name trains. Some of the K4 Pacifics bumped migrated to New Jersey to run out their last miles on the PRR's North Jersey Coast Line.
Photo/Robert J. Wayner Collection**

The demands of World War II strained the resources of all the nation's railroads to the limit. The manufacture of new streamlined trains had to be delayed until the war was over. Gasoline rationing caused a surge of passengers to the rails and the resulting crowded conditions disillusioned many. Uncomfortable conditions in troop sleepers also left a less than nostalgic feeling toward rail travel.

Improved roads and a burgeoning airline industry stressing bigger, better and faster aircraft made Pullman travel, particularly for businessmen, less attractive. Both the New York Central and the Pennsylvania rose to meet these post war challenges.

CO-OPERATION.....

One of the first postwar improvements was establishment of transcontinental sleeping car service, which went into effect in 1946. Through New York to Los Angeles sleepers were carried on the *Broadway Limited* from New York to Chicago where they were switched to the Santa Fe *Chief* for the run to Los Angeles. The *Chief* also carried through

LEFT: ABBA F3 diesels lead the Santa Fe *Chief* at Victorville, CA in 1950. Train carried a through sleeper from the Broadway Limited to Los Angeles.
Photo/Stan Kistler

BELOW: Santa Fe 4-4-2 sleeper Mohave was assigned to *Broadway Limited/Chief* transcontinental service in 1950. Seen at Clovis, NM, February 23, 1963.
Photo/J.B. McCall

sleepers from the *Twentieth Century* and through Washington, DC sleepers from the B&O's *Capitol Limited*. Other through routes to the west coast were established with other western railroads, but the *Broadway Limited* only exchanged through cars with the *Chief*.

Effective January 10, 1954, transcontinental sleepers were switched from the *Chief* to the *Super Chief*. The *Chief* started service on September 14, 1928 and was the Santa Fe's most deluxe Pullman train until the introduction of the *Super Chief* in 1937. In 1946 the *Chief* was running on a forty-eight hour schedule between Chicago and Los Angeles. Three hours were alloted for transfer of transcontinental sleepers from the *Broadway*, *Century* and *Capitol*.

TRANSCONTINENTAL SLEEPING CAR SERVICE ON THE BROADWAY LIMITED AND SANTA FE CHIEF

A 1950 PRR New York Division Consist Book listed the following sleepers assigned to New York-Los Angeles through service:

4 Cpt - 4 DBR - 2DR:

NASLINI   (AT&SF)
POLACCA   (AT&SF)
MOHAVE   (AT&SF)
TCHIREGE   (AT&SF)
IMPERIAL PASS   (PRR)
IMPERIAL PARK   (PRR)
IMPERIAL POINT   (PRR)

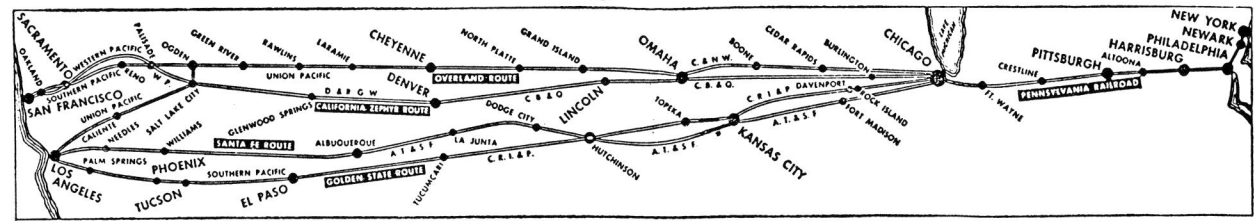

Table A **Coast-to-Coast Through Sleeping Car Service**

The Broadway Limited was re-equipped with more modern postwar cars, making its first revenue runs on March 15, 1949. A PRR 1950 consist book listed the following equipment assigned to train No. 28, the eastbound *Broadway*:

1 BM7OM (Baggage-Mail)
1 SL 4Cpt-4DBR-2DR
  (from Los Angeles)
1 SL 21 Roomette
1 SL 21 Roomette
1 SL SUPSR-4DBR
1 SL 4Cpt-4DBR-2DR
1 SL Lge 2DBR-Bar
1 Diner
1 Kitchen-Dorm
1 SL 4Cpt-4DBR-2DR
1 SL 10 Rmt-6DBR
1 SL 10 Rmt-6DBR
1 SL 10 Rmt-6DBR
1 SL 10 Rmt-6DBR
1 SL-OBS-MR-1DBR-Bar Lounge

ABOVE: Map and schedule of PRR-ATSF transcontinental sleeping car service; from September 30, 1951 PRR system passenger timetable.
Joel Rosenbaum Collection

The inauguration of through coast to coast sleeper service on the PRR and AT&SF on March 31, 1946, was not the first PRR transcontinental service. On January 4, 1892, the PRR established a through once-weekly sleeping car between New York and San Francisco. This service was withdrawn by the end of February of the same year due to a lack of patronage.

.....AND COMPETITION!

The Baltimore & Ohio Railroad provided competition for the Pennsylvania with through sleeping car between New York and Chicago. The B&O was somewhat at a disadvantage, as its New York patrons had to travel to Jersey City to board the trains, but the enterprising B&O inaugurated direct bus service from New York hotels and business locations to trainside.

The B&O would prove to be more of a competitor for Baltimore and Washington passengers destined for Chicago, and the *Capitol Limited* generally bested Pennsy's Washington *Broadway* connection in ridership by a hefty margin.

RIGHT: Timetable showing Baltimore & Ohio New York City-Chicago through passenger service; from the July 1957 *Official Railway Guide*.

ABOVE: B&O #6, the *Capitol Limited* departs Chicago's Grand Central Station on May 19, 1961 enroute to Washington with a sixteen car consist which included two domes and an observation lounge. By this date through service to New York (Jersey City) had been discontinued. LEFT: Observation lounge *Dana* brings up markers of the westbound *Capitol Limited* at the B&O station in Connellsville, PA on October 20, 1966.

Two Kodachromes/Robert Malinoski

An EMD E7 A and B set power the westbound *Twentieth Century Limited* as Oscawanna, New York on July 28, 1947. The "new" 1948 Century was still a year away.   Photo/George E. Votava

Pullman sleeper-lounge-observation *Bedloes Island* brings up markers of westbound Train 25, the New York Central's *Twentieth Century Limited*, at Oscawanna, New York on July 28, 1947. New equipment would be assigned to this train beginning September 15, 1948.

Photo/George E. Votava

The New York Central inaugurated a brand new *Twentieth Century Limited* on September 15, 1948. It was dedicated by General Dwight D. Eisenhower, then President of Columbia University, at ceremonies held trackside in Grand Central Station. In his remarks, the General heaped praise on the New York Central and the entire railroad industry, stating:

"I congratulate the New York Central System and the entire railroad industry upon this example of high standards of achievement and progress. It is this kind of technological progress that keeps America in the forefront of nations."

A beribboned bottle containing water from the Hudson and Mohawk Rivers, Lake Erie and Lake Michigan, all bodies of water along the route of the *Century*, was broken against the end of the new train's observation car.

The westbound *Twentieth Century Limited* swings around the curve at Spuyten Duyvil in August, 1963. Coaches comprise the forward part of the formerly all-Pullman New York Central flagship.   FACING PAGE: Sleeper lounge observation *Hickory Creek* brings up markers of the 17-car consist.

Two Kodachromes/Robert Malinoski

FACING PAGE: The *Broadway Limited* rolls into Eglewood, Illinois in 1965 behind triple Pennsy E8A's. Lead unit 5898 survives today-- in as-delivered PRR pinstripe livery-- on the Blue Mountain & Reading Railroad at Hamburg, Pennsylvania.
Photo/Jim Boyd

ABOVE: PRR Train 29-- The *Broadway*-- glides through Tacony, Pennsylvania on a weekday evening in July, 1966, with observation-lounge *Mountain View* bringing up the markers, BELOW.
Two photos/William J. Coxey

LEFT: PRR observation car *Samuel Rea* graces the rear of Train 28, the eastbound *Broadway Limited*, in Pennsylvania Station, New York City on July 27, 1965.
Kodachrome/Robert Malinoski

BELOW: Sleeper-lounge-observation *Mountain View* was part of the new postwar Broadway Limited consist which went into service March 15, 1949. Observation cars were removed from the *Broadway Limited* in December, 1967.

Photo/George E. Votava

RIGHT: The *Mountain View* is seen in Pennsylvania Station, New York at 10:10 A.M. March 26, 1966 having arrived on the eastbound *Broadway Limited*.
Kodachrome/Robert Malinoski

FOLLOWING TWO PAGES: Illustrations of Master Room features, from the brochure *New Type Room Accommodations in Sleeping Cars on the Pennsylvania Railroad*, published by the Pennsy in May, 1948.
Joel Rosenbaum Collection

MASTER ROOM-BEDROOM-OBSERVATION-BUFFET-LOUNGE CAR

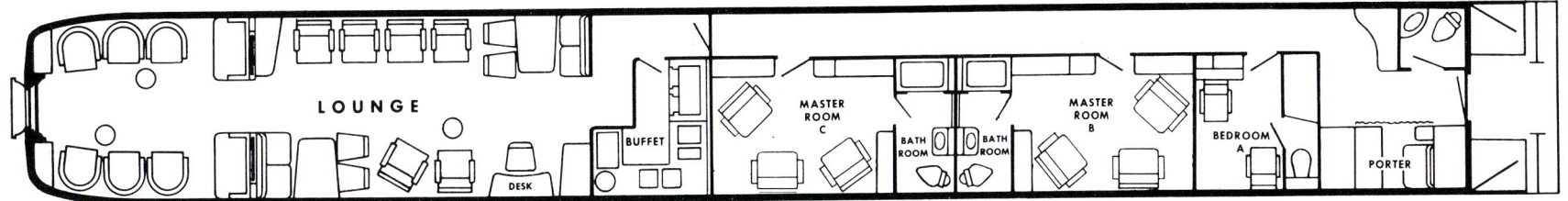

2 Master Rooms; 1 Double Bedroom (Parallel Type); 25 Lounge Passengers. Maximum Sleeping Occupancy—6 Persons

MASTER ROOM
For 1 or 2 Persons

Below are two sketches of the Master Room showing details of this accommodation in both day and night-time service. This stately accommodation has been modernized and continues to provide the ultimate in refined comfort and privacy for sleeping car passengers. Red lines pin-point outstanding features.

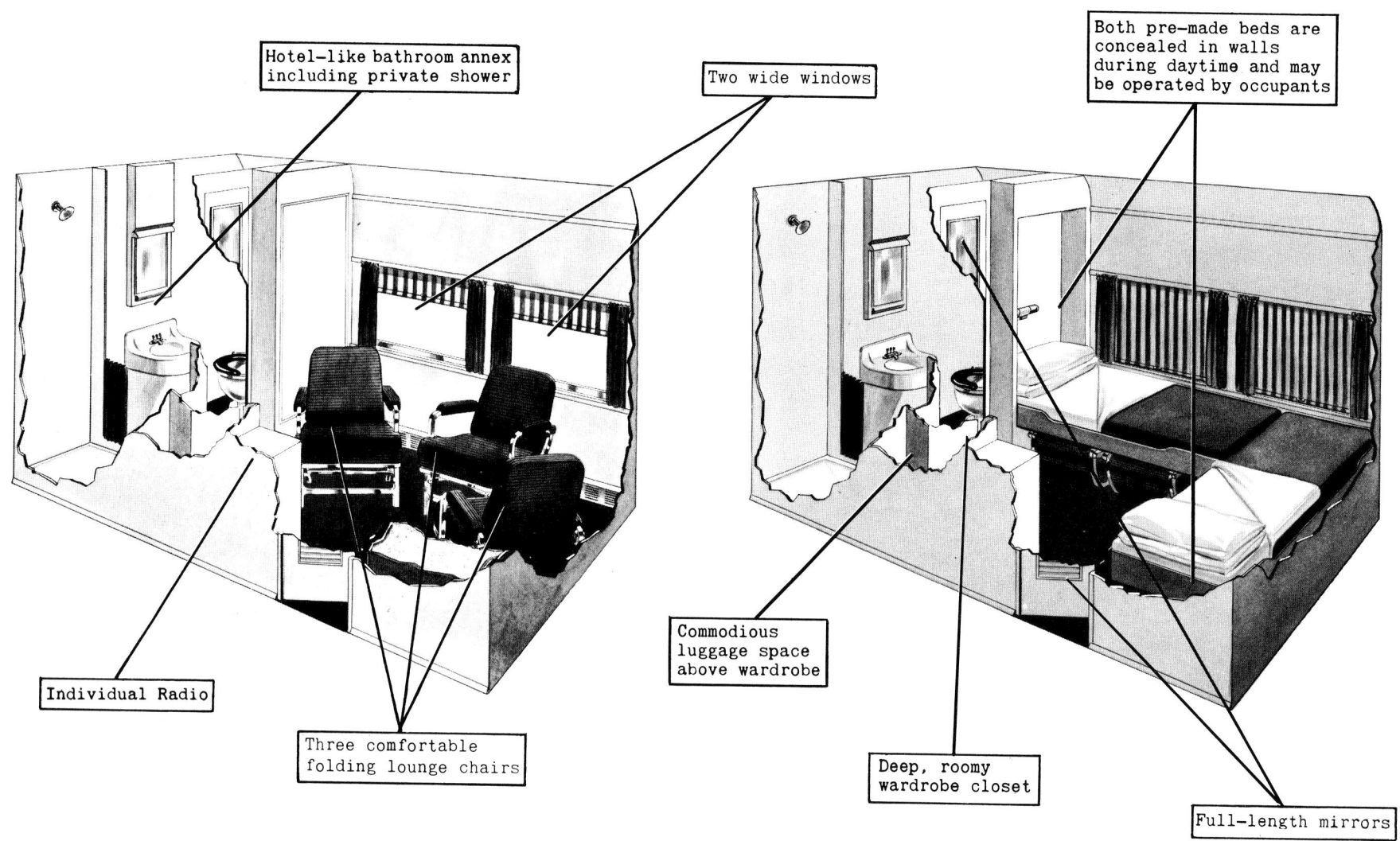

MASTER ROOM
For 1 or 2 Persons

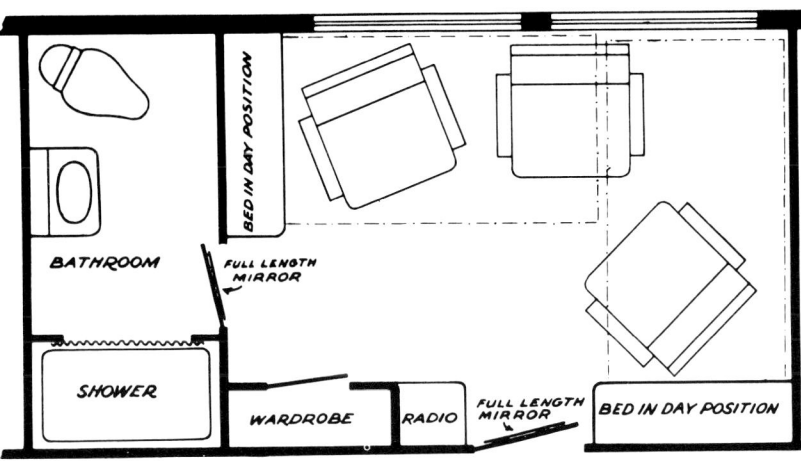

Above sketch shows floor plan of the modern Master Room accommodating 1 or 2 persons. Dotted lines show location of beds in night position. Lounge chairs may be folded and placed under beds at night thus affording additional space.

Daytime Features

- Toilet annex with complete bathroom facilities.
- Three comfortable folding lounge chairs are provided.
- Two windows allow free, wide-angle vision.
- Roomy wardrobe provides ample space for clothes.
- Two full-length mirrors.
- Beds may be lowered without porter's assistance—day or night.

Night-time Features

- Beds are pre-made, thus eliminating inconvenience and providing more privacy en route.
- Ample floor space after beds are lowered.
- Room temperature individually controlled by occupants—night and day.

See Floor Plan 10, Page 22 for location of Master Rooms in latest type sleeping cars.

Mountain View brings up markers on Train 29 as it enters Chicago Union Station in March, 1967, the last year of operation for the sleeper-lounge-observations. Kodachrome/Richard D. Forest

The 1950 PRR New York Division consist book listed the following sleepers by name and configuration assigned to trains 28 and 29:

21 Roomette:
Massillon Inn
Grand Rapids Inn
Ravenna Inn

10 Rmt-6DBR:
Manistee Rapids
Conemaugh Rapids
Little Miami Rapids
Clearfield Rapids
Catawissa Rapids
Clarion Rapids
Schuylkill Rapids

4 Cpt-4DBR-2DR:
Imperial Bower
Imperial Field
Imperial Terrain
Imperial Trees

12 Dup. SR -4 DBR
Cabin Creek
College Creek

2 DBR-Bar
Harbor Cove
Harbor Rest

2 MR-1 DBR OBSERVATION
Mountain View
Tower View

RIGHT: The *Broadway Limited* is seen near 49th Street in Chicago behind a pair of E8's in "pre-merger" livery, October 1967. Within four months the *Broadway* would be operating under Penn Central auspices. Kodachrome/Jim Boyd

BELOW: Illustrations from a *Broadway Limited* brochure issued by the Pennsy in 1953. Tom Gallo Collection

NO FINER RELAXATION

THE OBSERVATION-LOUNGE AND CLUB-LOUNGE CARS reflect in their styling and decorative harmony the restfulness that you enjoy on the *Broadway Limited*. Attractively furnished with soft-cushioned chairs and settees, refreshment buffets, game and writing tables, magazine libraries and many other refinements. Terminal Telephone Service is provided in Observation-Lounge in Chicago and New York for local calls. En route, Radio-Telephone service in Club-Lounge for local and long distance calls.

NO FINER WAY TO DINE

You will enjoy a notable experience in fine eating in the *Broadway's* dining car, in an atmosphere of charm and splendor. Here a wide choice of tempting dishes awaits your pleasure, many of them Pennsylvania Railroad's own specialties. Service is gracious... in the traditional *Broadway Limited* manner. Wide windows, colorful draperies and furnishings, individual table lamps and other distinctive appointments add further to your dining pleasure.

ALL-PRIVATE-ROOM FLEET LEADER

BROADWAY LIMITED

NEW YORK

PHILADELPHIA

CHICAGO

BROADWAY LIMITED dinner menu of November, 1967 still offered five entrees. Check that Oxtail Soup...or how 'bout Roast Prime Rib au jus...for just $5.95!
E.L. Pardee collection

Broadway Limited

DINNER

For private room meal service a charge of one dollar per person will be made. Immediate service cannot be assured.

A La Carte

appetizers

Oxtail Soup .50	Medley of Fresh Fruit with Strawberries .60
Beef Consomme, Vermicelli .50	Pimento with Anchovies .75
Pate de Maison .85	Chilled Tomato Juice .50

prepared to order

Emince of Turkey and Mushrooms in Paprika Sauce with Sherry, Rice Pilaf, Vegetable du Jour, Choice of Dessert, Pot of Coffee 4.25

Minced Ham Omelette, Parsley Potato, Fresh Asparagus, Lettuce Heart, French Dressing, Choice of Dessert, Pot of Coffee 3.85

salad

Lettuce and Tomato, French Dressing .85

desserts

Chocolate Cake .60	Apple Pie .60
Caramel Custard .60	Fig Compote .60
Vanilla Ice Cream with Pineapple Sauce .60	
Camembert, Roquefort or Gruyere Cheese, Crackers .60	

beverages

Pot of Coffee .50	Grade "A" Milk .30
Pot of Tea .50	Instant Decaffeinated Coffee .50

May we suggest serving with your Dinner tonight

Manhattan or Extra Dry Martini Cocktail 1.00

Burgundy Wine (half bottle) 3.00

White Graves Wine (half bottle) 2.50

Welcome!

Bon Appetit!

The BROADWAY LIMITED bids you welcome to its table. Enjoy the renowned Continental and American cuisine of the Line's master chefs ... the courteous service of its most skilled waiters. In this dining car — pride of the Pennsylvania — we are dedicated to making your repast aboard an exquisite dining experience. Your comments to the steward are solicited.

Sidney N. Phelps
Manager, Dining Car Service

Where do Broadway travelers find the morning paper? In their shoe box. Compliments of the Pennsy.

Table D'Hote

(PLEASE WRITE ON MEAL CHECK EACH ITEM DESIRED)

Green Olives	Radishes	Iced Celery

Oxtail Soup	Medley of Fresh Fruit with Strawberries
Beef Consomme, Vermicelli	Pimento with Anchovies
Pate de Maison	Chilled Tomato Juice

*GRILLED SHAD FILET, MAITRE D'HOTEL 5.85

*BREAST OF CORNISH HEN A LA KIEV 5.95

ROAST PRIME RIBS OF BEEF AU JUS 5.95

*BROILED BONELESS SIRLOIN STEAK, FRIED ONION RINGS 6.95

*CALF'S LIVER SAUTE WITH BACON 5.85

*These entrees are prepared to order

Parsley Potato	Fresh Asparagus, Drawn Butter
Lyonnaise Potatoes	Buttered String Beans

Lettuce, Chicory, Romaine, Tomato Salad, French Dressing

Muffins from Carrier

Chocolate Cake	Apple Pie
Caramel Custard	Fig Compote
Camembert, Roquefort or Gruyere Cheese, Crackers	
Vanilla Ice Cream with Pineapple Sauce	

Pot of Coffee	Instant Decaffeinated Coffee
Pot of Tea	Grade "A" Milk

Mints

Pennsylvania Railroad

ABOVE: IN THE PENN CENTRAL ERA, the westbound *Broadway Limited* approaches the C&O diamond at Hanna, Indiana in September, 1970. Kodachrome/Mike Schafer

FACING PAGE: Illustrations of car floorplans from *New Type Room Accommodations in Sleeping Cars on the Pennsylvania Railroad*, published by the Pennsy in May, 1948. **Tom Gallo Collection**

BEDROOM-BUFFET-LOUNGE CAR

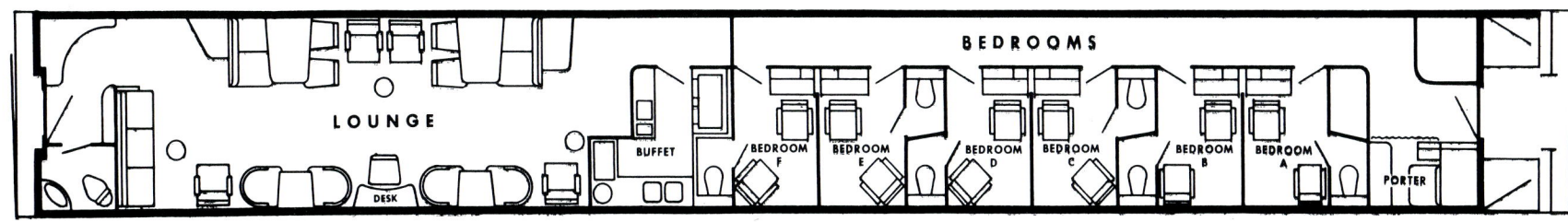

6 Double Bedrooms (Parallel Type); 20 Lounge Passengers. Maximum Sleeping Occupancy—12 Persons

BEDROOM-DRAWING ROOM-BUFFET-LOUNGE CAR

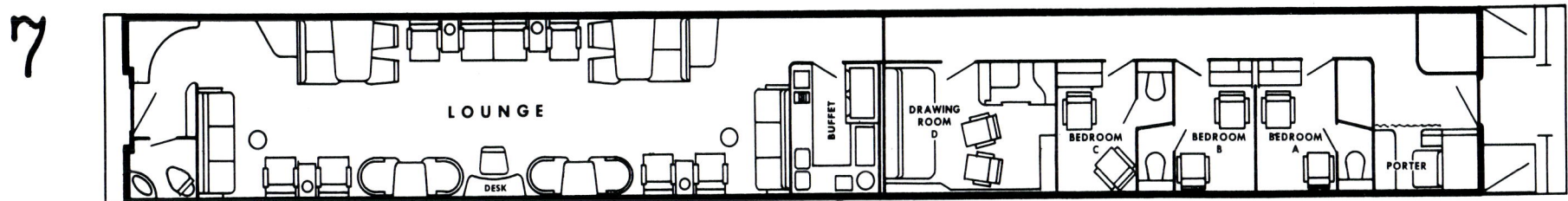

3 Double Bedrooms (Parallel Type); 1 Drawing Room; 27 Lounge Passengers. Maximum Sleeping Occupancy—9 Persons

BEDROOM-BUFFET-LOUNGE CAR

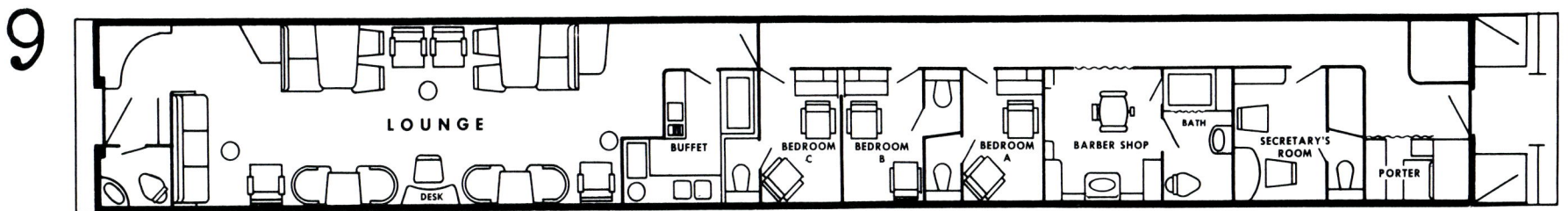

3 Double Bedrooms (Parallel Type); 1 Secretary's Room; 1 Barber Shop; 20 Lounge Passengers
Maximum Sleeping Occupancy—6 Persons

FACING PAGE, TOP: Penn Central has had its fling with passenger service, but sleeper *Kaskaskia Rapids* is still in Pennsy Tuscan livery. The date is April 23, 1971, and one week later Amtrak will become the operator of the *Broadway Limited* and most other surviving long-distance trains in the United States.

FACING PAGE, BOTTOM: Pennsy sleeper-lounge *Larch Falls* clatters over the diamonds at 21st Street in Chicago in the consist of an eastbound *Broadway Limited,* April 24, 1971. Note the toast being raised in the second window from the right-- perhaps a good riddance to the Penn Central era.
Two Kodachromes/Tom Nemeth

ABOVE: Twin-unit diner operating in the *Broadway Limited* consist in September, 1967.

RIGHT: Seldom-photographed Broadway sleeper observation lounge *Tower View* departs Chicago in September, 1967.
Two Kodachromes/Richard D. Forest

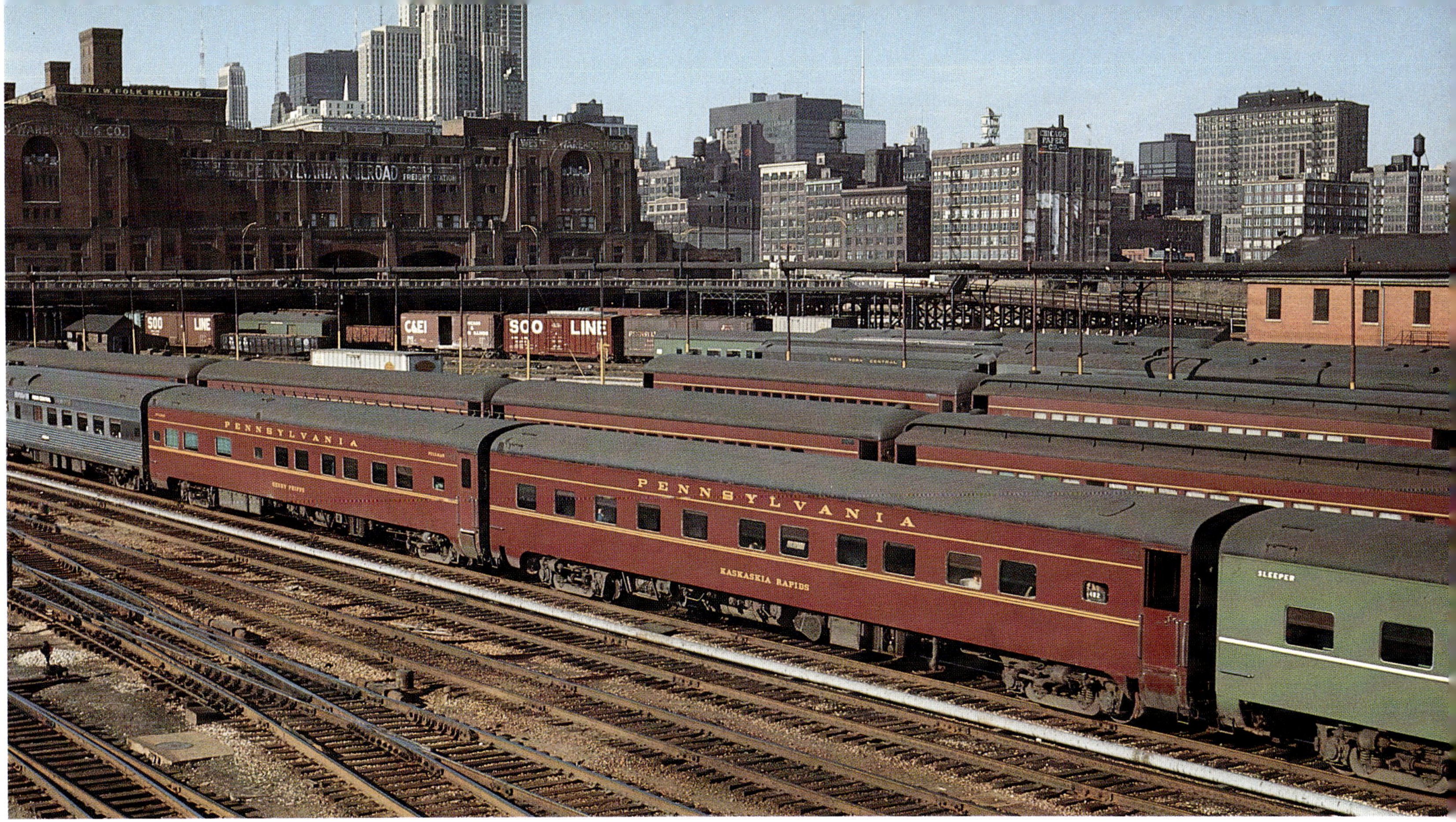
PENNSYLVANIA RAILROAD
SOO LINE
SOO LINE
C&EI
PENNSYLVANIA
PENNSYLVANIA
KASKASKIA RAPIDS
SLEEPER

PENNSYLVANIA
LARCH FALLS

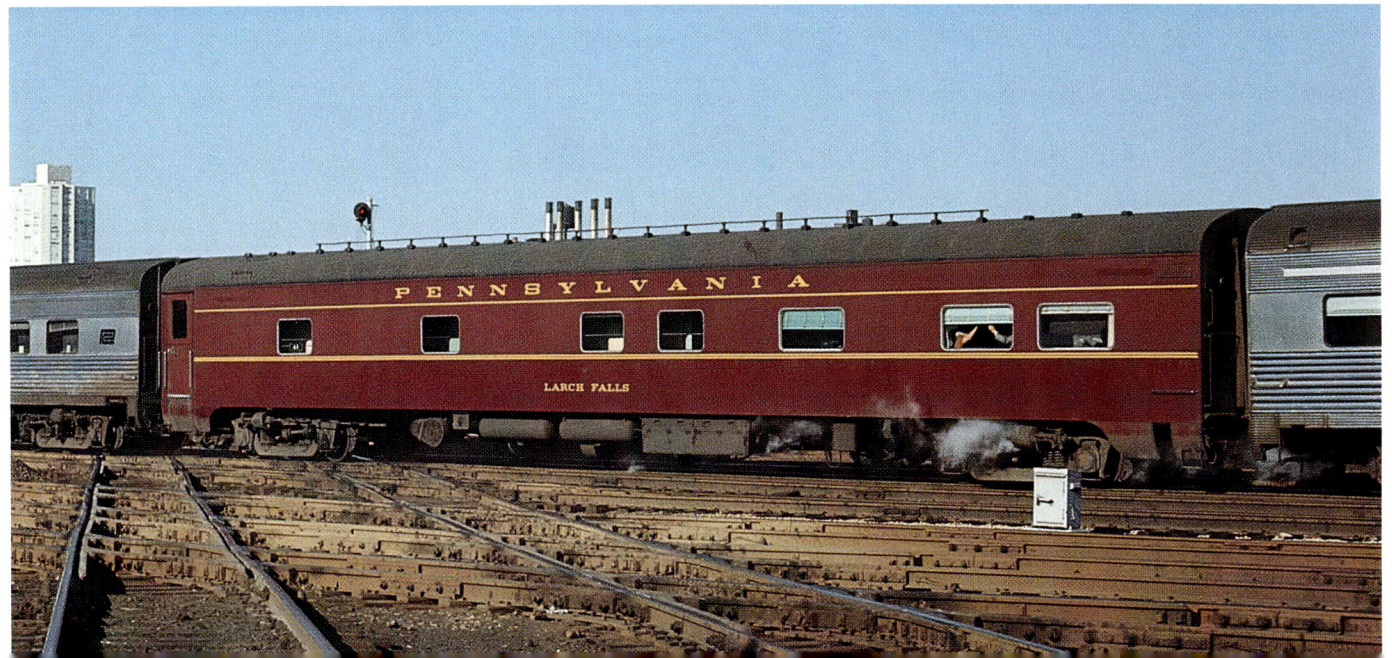

EAST/WEST TIMETABLE

Effective January 10, 1971

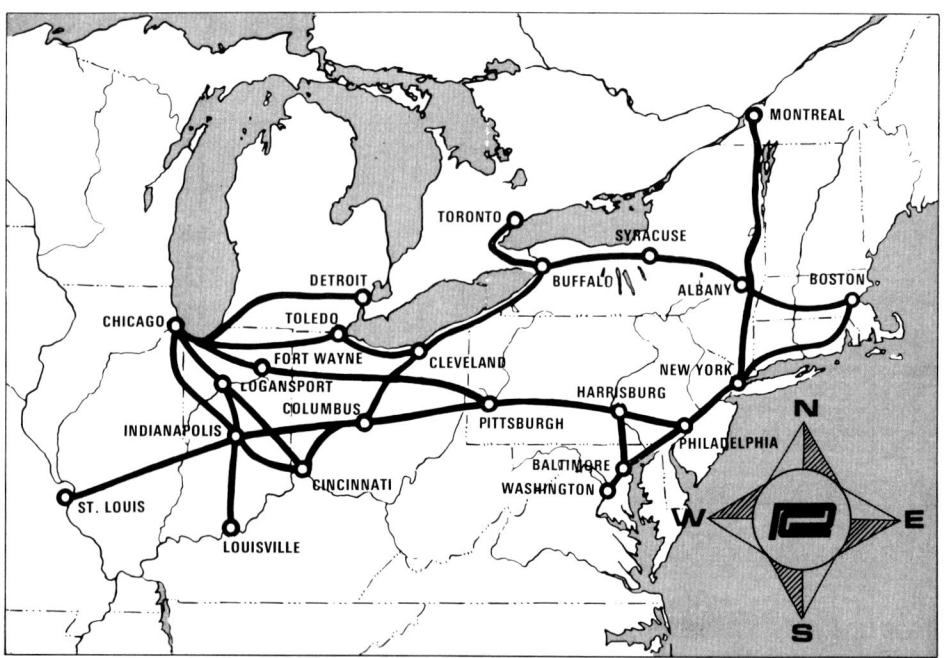

ABOVE and RIGHT: Penn Central East-West passenger schedule, which listed both former PRR and NYC services. Even under Penn Central the timecard still showed three New York-Chicago services via Pittsburgh.

FACING PAGE: Penn Central breakfast menu from the *Broadway Limited*, issued May 20, 1970-- the last full year of Penn Central operation of the famed train.

Tom Gallo Collection

			25	33	23	31	49	55	13	53
			The Duquesne	The Juniata	Manhattan Limited	"Spirit of St. Louis" 31-77 Cincinnati Limited	Broadway Limited	Pennsylvania Limited		Note 2
Miles		LOCAL TIME	Daily	Daily	Daily	Daily	Daily	Daily	Except Mon.	Daily
			AM	AM	PM	PM	PM	PM	AM	AM
0	Lv	NEW YORK (Pa. Sta.)..(ET)	7 35	U11 45	1 30	4 05	4 55	9 25		
10	"	Newark	7 50	U12 00	1 45	R 4 22	R 5 11	R 9 41		
58	"	Trenton	8 35	U12 50	2 31	R 5 10	R 5 55			
85	"	PHILADELPHIA								
		North Phila. Station	9 06		R 3 02	R 5 37	R 6 21			
		Penn Cent. Sta. (30th St.)		2 05				R11 28		
111	Lv	Paoli	9 40	2 33	3 40	6 09	6 53	11 56		
130	"	Coatesville	10 02	2 53	4 00	6 54	7 40	12 48		
159	"	Lancaster	10 32	3 23	4 27	7 27	8 11	1 20		
194	Ar	Harrisburg	11 15	3 55	5 03					
0	Lv	Washington				A 5 00				
40	"	Baltimore (P. C. Sta.)				A 5 55				
123	Ar	Harrisburg				A 8 10				
194	Lv	Harrisburg	11 35	4 05	5 20	7 27	8 21			
255	"	Lewistown (Pa. State Univ.*)	12 46	5 15	6 31	8 48		1 40		
279	"	Mount Union			6 54					
291	"	Huntingdon	1 21		7 10					
311	"	Tyrone	1 51		7 40					
325	"	Altoona	2 13	6 35	8 02	10 08	10 52	4 07		
362	Lv	Johnstown	3 22	7 42	9 10		11 58	5 16		
399	"	Latrobe	4 12		9 58			6 02		
408	"	Greensburg	4 25		10 11			6 19		
432	"	Wilkinsburg	D 5 05	D 9 07	10 46			6 50		
439	Ar	PITTSBURGH (P. C. Sta.)	5 20	9 20	11 05		1 31	7 05		
439	Lv	PITTSBURGH (P. C. Sta.)			11 30		1 31	7 35		11 45
451	"	Sewickley			11 48					12 21
465	"	Rochester			12 05					12 27
469	"	Beaver Falls			12 13			8 11		12 54
489	"	East Palestine						8 57		1 16
508	"	Salem			1 03					
522	Lv	Alliance			1 22			9 17		1 36
541	"	Canton			1 50			9 45		2 06
548	"	Massillon								2 20
563	"	Orrville								2 37
574	"	Wooster			F 2 25			10 24		2 52
614	"	Mansfield			3 08			11 10		3 40
628	"	Crestline			3 30			11 28		3 58
640	Lv	Bucyrus						11 47		
657	"	Upper Sandusky								4 32
685	"	Ada								5 05
700	"	Lima			4 41			12 38		5 20
727	"	Van Wert					6 16	1 03		5 47
759	Ar	FORT WAYNE			5 40		7 11	1 35		6 20
799	Lv	Warsaw			6 21			2 18		7 04
823	"	Plymouth (ET)						2 38		7 24
864	"	Valparaiso (CT)			P 6 20		7 42	2 14		7 05
882	"	Gary (5th & Chase Sts.)					D 8 02	2 32		7 25
900	Ar	Englewood			D 7 05		D 8 25	D 2 52		
907	Ar	CHICAGO (Union Sta.) (CT)			7 25		8 40	3 10		8 05
439	Lv	PITTSBURGH (P.C. Sta.)(ET)				1 05			10 00	
482	"	Steubenville				2 17				
529	"	Dennison				3 43				
561	"	Coshocton				4 20				
597	"	Newark				5 13				
630	Ar	COLUMBUS							2 05	
630	Lv	COLUMBUS				6 00				
675	"	Springfield				6 50				
700	"	Dayton				7 30				
721	"	Middletown				8 02				
752	Ar	CINCINNATI (Union Term.)				9 00				
630	Lv	Columbus				5 40			2 05	
684	"	Xenia				F 6 42				
700	"	Dayton				7 05			3 58	
742	"	Richmond				8 05			5 03	
810	Ar	INDIANAPOLIS				9 55			6 38	
810	Lv	INDIANAPOLIS				9 55			6 38	
849	"	Greencastle				F11 00			T 7 40	
882	"	Terre Haute (ET)				11 40			8 15	
950	"	Effingham (CT)				11 45			8 30	
1047	Ar	East St. Louis				B 1 15			B10 10	
1030	Ar	ST. LOUIS (CT)				1 35			10 30	
			PM	PM	AM	PM	AM	PM	PM	PM

Broadway Limited

A La Carte

Chilled Orange Juice .60   Melon in Season .60
Cooked Prunes .60   Cooked or Dry Cereal .60
Tomato or Prune Juice .60

Toasted English Muffins (2) .60
Muffins (3), Butter and Preserves .60
White Toast (3 slices), Butter and Preserves .60

Pot of Tea .60
Pot of Coffee .60
Individual Half Pint Milk .30
Instant Decaffeinated Coffee .60

Combinations

$2.20
Choice of Fruit, Juice or Cereal
(Listed under A la Carte)
Boiled, Fried or Scrambled Eggs
Toast or Muffins
Butter and Preserves
Pot of Coffee

$1.85
Choice of Fruit or Juice
(Listed under A la Carte)
Cooked or Dry Cereal
Muffins (3) or Toast (2 slices)
Butter and Preserves
Pot of Coffee

BREAKFAST

(PLEASE WRITE ON MEAL CHECK EACH ITEM DESIRED)

For private room meal service a charge of one dollar per person will be made. Immediate service cannot be assured.

Bon Appetit!

The BROADWAY LIMITED bids you welcome to its table. Enjoy the renowned Continental and American cuisine of the Line's master chefs ... the courteous service of its most skilled waiters. In this dining car — pride of the Penn Central — we are dedicated to making your repast aboard an exquisite dining experience.

Table D'Hote

$2.50

Cooked Prunes   Oatmeal
Cream of Wheat   Melon in Season
Crisp Dry Cereal   Chilled Orange Juice
Tomato or Prune Juice
(Any two items listed above will be served for .30 additional)

SAUSAGE LINKS WITH SCRAMBLED EGGS
BROWNED CORNED BEEF HASH, POACHED EGG
BROILED SUGAR CURED HAM WITH EGGS
WHEAT CAKES, BACON AND SYRUP
COUNTRY BACON WITH EGGS

Home Fried Potatoes served on request

White, Rye or Whole Wheat Toast
Toasted English Muffin - Sweet Rolls - Muffins

Preserves   Orange Marmalade

Coffee   Grade "A" Milk   Tea
Instant Decaffeinated Coffee

THE STEWARD WILL WELCOME YOUR COMMENTS ON OUR FOOD AND SERVICE
IF YOU PREFER, WRITE TO SIDNEY N. PHELPS, DIRECTOR, DINING, SLEEPING AND
PARLOR CAR SERVICE, PENN CENTRAL, LONG ISLAND CITY, N.Y. 11101

PC-2
5-20-70

PENN CENTRAL

LEFT: Penn Central E8A 4276 makes a less than flattering statement for Penn Central. The peeling, unlettered unit leads an eight car *Broadway Limited* out of Chicago Union Station on April 24, 1971.

BELOW: The *Broadway Limited* never attained an all-Penn Central identity, but several sleepers and coaches were repainted in PC's pea soup green. Car 4350, *Octoraro Rapids* is seen crossing the diamonds at 21st Street in Chicago, April 23, 1971

Two Kodachromes/Tom Nemeth

ABOVE: Amtrak was but thirteen months old when Penn Central E8 4286 and three sisters growled across the diamonds at 21st street in Chicago with the *Broadway Limited*. The trailing E unit and several coaches already bore the markings of the National Railroad Passenger Corporation.
Kodachrome/Mike Schafer

LEFT: One week before Amtrak-Day, Penn Central E8 4291 (still in Pennsy Tuscan) leads the eastbound *Broadway Limited* through 21st Street Interlocking, just minutes out of Chicago Union Station. The date is April 24, 1971.
Kodachrome/Tom Nemeth

Penn Central GG1's 4920 and 4910 make a brief stop with a thirteen car consist at Paoli station on Philadelphia's "Main Line" in June, 1970. It was a long standing tradition to use two G's on the *Broadway,* even into the Penn Central era.
Photo/William J. Coxey

The ignominy that was Penn Central began in Philadelphia on the cold and overcast night of February 1, 1968.

Penn Central continued to operate the *Broadway*, with little fanfare. A few sleepers and coaches received the pea-soup green of the new company, but by March of 1970, Penn Central had showed its hand concerning the future of the *Broadway Limited* and all other New York-Chicago passenger runs: it wanted out.

The *Broadway Limited* would hang on for another fourteen months until May 1, 1971 when the newly formed National Railroad Passenger Corporation-- Amtrak-- arrived on the scene to assume its financial responsibility.

PENN CENTRAL

Train 49, the westbound Penn Central *Broadway Limited*, is seen at speed east of Monmouth Junction, NJ on September 1, 1970. GG1's 4902 and 4925 have a fourteen car consist of one baggage, six sleepers (including *Penns Rapids, Fishing Rapids, Sam Kier* and *Larch Falls*), one twin-unit diner, a tavern lounge, and four coaches.
Photo/David L. Hill

The decline of rail passenger traffic in the 1950's led both the New York Central and the Pennsylvania to eliminate some of their long distance passenger trains as well as some local runs. The Central combined its *Commodore Vanderbilt* with *The Twentieth Century Limited* in the late 1950's with the result that *The Century* was no longer an all-Pullman extra fare train. Coaches were added and *The Century* lost all the prestige it once had.

LEFT: Amtrak SDP40F refueling at Crestline, Ohio on the eastbound *Broadway Limited*, **June 3, 1974. The big SDP40F's served Trains 40 and 41 for only a brief period in the mid-1970's.**

Kodachrome/Preston Cook

BELOW: Amtrak operated an observation car on the *Broadway Limited* **for a short period after assuming operation of the train from Penn Central. A sleeper-lounge-observation brings up** *Broadway* **markers at Fort Wayne, Indiana in June, 1972.**

Kodachrome/Mike Schafer

Chapter Five:

Amtrak Takes The Throttle

The Broadway Limited benefited from the downgrading of the *Century*. Extra Pullmans were added to the *Broadway's* consist. The PRR upgraded the train, and at one point it was expanded to as many as twenty cars.

On December 2, 1967 *The Century* pulled out of Grand Central Station for the last time. A little less than two weeks later, on December 12, 1967, the *Broadway Limited* left Pennsylvania Station for the last time as an all-Pullman train. Beginning on December 13, 1967, *The Broadway* was consolidated with *The General* and coaches were added. The consolidated train continued to carry the name *Broadway Limited*, but it was renumbered as trains 48 and 49, which were originally *The General's* train numbers. With this consolidation, the observation cars were removed from the *Broadway Limited*.

UPPER RIGHT: The Amtrak *Broadway Limited* **races westward across the Pennsy "High Line" in Secacus, New Jersey at 5:15 P.M. September 10, 1973. GG1 4938 is in charge of a 14 car consist which includes a Penn Central business car (in Amtrak livery), baggage, two slumbercoaches, four coaches, lounge, twin-unit diner, and three coaches. View is from the New Jersey Turnpike at Snake Hill.**
Kodachrome/Robert Malinoski

RIGHT: By the 1980's, Amtrak's most modern electric power-- AEM-7's-- handled the *Broadway* **in and out of New York City. Motor 912 glides through the reverse curve in Elizabeth, New Jersey on 3 Track, March 28, 1981.**
Kodachrome/Don Jilson

EAST—WEST SERVICE

NEW YORK
PHILADELPHIA
WASHINGTON
HARRISBURG
CLEVELAND
CHICAGO
ST. LOUIS
KANSAS CITY

AND INTERMEDIATE STATIONS

also

PHILADELPHIA—HARRISBURG

CHICAGO—FLORIDA

CHICAGO—CINCINNATI

NEWPORT NEWS

CHICAGO—DETROIT

NATIONAL RAILROAD PASSENGER CORPORATION

Amtrak

TRAIN SCHEDULES

NOTICE
THE INTERCITY TRAINS SHOWN HEREIN ARE OPERATED BY THE PENN CENTRAL TRANSPORTATION COMPANY UNDER CONTRACT FOR THE NATIONAL RAILROAD PASSENGER CORPORATION

Form 1   Effective July 12, 1971

		600	4	48	602	604	606	608	618	610	612	16	614
EAST via PITTSBURGH TO WASHINGTON HARRISBURG PHILADELPHIA NEW YORK and Intermediate Stations	LOCAL TIME	Except Sat. & Sun. H	"Spirit of St Louis" Daily	Broadway Limited Daily	H	Except Sundays Daily	H	Except Sat. & Sun. H	Except Sundays H	Daily	Except Saturdays H	Except Sat. & Sun. H	The Duquesne Daily	Daily
		AM	AM	PM	AM	AM	AM	PM	PM	PM	PM	PM	PM
Lv CHICAGO (Union Station)......(CT)				4 00									
" Gary............................(CT)				R 4 33									
" Fort Wayne....................(ET)				6 18									
" Lima...........................				8 20									
Lv Crestline......................				9 31									
" Canton.........................				F11 10									
Ar PITTSBURGH (P. C. Sta.).......(ET)				1 06									
Lv KANSAS CITY (Mo Pac 16).......(CT)			5 40										
" Warrensburg....................			6 47										
" Sedalia........................			7 25										
" Jefferson City..................			8 37										
" Kirkwood......................			10 35										
Ar ST. LOUIS.....................			11 15										
Lv ST. LOUIS........P. C........(CT)			11 35										
" Effingham......................			1 15										
" Terre Haute....................(ET)			2 20										
Lv Indianapolis..................(ET)			3 55										
" Richmond......................			5 15										
" Dayton.........................			7 05										
" Columbus......................			8 30										
Ar PITTSBURGH (Penn Cent. Sta.)...			12 35										
Lv PITTSBURGH (Penn Cent. Sta.)..(ET)			12 35	1 06								12 30	
" Wilkinsburg....................												12 40	
" Greensburg.....................												1 12	
" Latrobe........................												1 25	
" Johnstown......................												2 07	
Lv Altoona.......................			3 19	3 43								3 10	
" Tyrone.........................												3 30	
" Huntingdon.....................												3 59	
" Lewistown (Pa. State Univ.).....			4 35									4 40	
Ar HARRISBURG..................			5 55	6 11								5 50	
Lv Harrisburg.....................			V 6 40	V 6 40									
Ar Baltimore (Penn Cent. Sta.).....			DV9 15	DV9 15									
" WASHINGTON................			V 9 55	V 9 55									
Lv HARRISBURG..................		5 41	• 6 29	6 29	6 50	8 00	10 05	12 35	3 00	4 25	5 25	6 00	7 55
" Middletown.....................						8 16		K12 51		4 41	5 40		
" Elizabethtown...................		5 58									5 47		K 8 11
" Mount Joy......................											5 54		
" Lancaster.......................		6 15	7 • 01	7 01	7 22	8 33	10 37	1 07	3 33	4 58	6 07	6 38	8 27
" Parkesburg.....................					Y 7 43								
" Coatesville.....................		6 41			7 49	8 59	11 03	1 35	3 59	5 24		6 32	7 10	8 53
" Downingtown..................		6 48			7 55	9 05	11 09	1 39	4 05	5 30		6 38		8 59
" Whitford.......................		6 53			8 00	F 9 10							
" Malvern........................		7 00			Y 8 06	F 9 16							
" Paoli...........................		D 7 04	D 7 • 48	D 7 48	D 8 09	9 19	11 22	1 51	4 17	5 42	6 50	7 29	9 11
" Berwyn........................													
" Wayne.........................													
" Rosemont......................													
" Bryn Mawr.....................													
" Ardmore.......................												5 55	7 03
" Narberth.......................													
" Overbrook......................													
Ar PHILADELPHIA													
" Penn Central Sta. (30th St.).....		7 29			8 34	9 44	11 50	2 18	4 41	6 06	7 14		9 34
" Penn Center....................		7 33			8 38	9 48	11 54	2 22	4 45	6 10	7 18		9 38
Lv Penn Central Sta. (30th St.).....	X 8 00	D 8 • 21	D 8 21	X 9 00	X10 • 15	X12 14	X 3 00	X 5 13	X 6 19			7 56	
" North Phila. Sta................		D 8 • 48	D 8 48	X 9 40	X10 • 54	X12 51	X 3 38	X 5 51	XE6 55			8 24	
" Trenton.........................		D 9 • 34	D 9 34	X10 32	X11 • 45	X 1 35	X 4 23	X 6 34	X 7 07			9 09	
" Newark.........................	X 9 18			X10 47	X12 • 00	X 1 50	X 4 40	X 6 50	X 7 55			D 9 19	
Ar NEW YORK (Penna. Sta.)......(ET)	X 9 35	9 • 50	9 50									9 25	
		AM	AM	AM	AM	NOON	PM	PM	PM	PM	PM	PM	PM

REFERENCE NOTES

Limited checked baggage service available. Consult ticket agents.
♦ The State of Michigan and certain cities in the State of Indiana do not observe advance time. Time shown at this point conforms to local time.
♣ Tickets from this station available only on train.
CT Central Time. ET Eastern Time.
• Train No. 48 from Harrisburg to New York.
△ Except Sundays and Sept. 6.
D Stops only to discharge passengers.
E Except Sundays.

F Stops only on signal to receive or discharge passengers.
H Will not run Sept. 6.
K Stops Saturdays only.
R Stops only to receive passengers.
V Train No. 548 from Harrisburg to Washington.
X Connecting train. Passengers change trains at Penn Central Station (30th St.), Philadelphia.
Y Stops Mondays thru Fridays except Sept. 6.

One of the earliest Amtrak New York-Chicago passenger schedules, effective July 12, 1971. Compare with Penn Central schedule of January 10, 1971, which appears on page 68. Amtrak New York-Chicago service via Pittsburgh had been cut to one train-- the *Broadway Limited*.

Tom Gallo Collection

The Penn-Central revealed its long haul passenger service plans in March of 1970 when the road sought to eliminate all of its NY-Chicago and NY-St. Louis passenger trains.

The future of all long distance passenger trains in the United States looked bleak. Congress wrestled with the problem, proposing legislation, originally known as Railpax (or "rail peace") to relieve the private railroads of the financial burden of operating intercity passenger service. President Nixon signed legislation creating the National Railroad Passenger Corporation, known as AMTRAK, which came into existence on May 1, 1971. Its purpose was to save was was left of American intercity passenger service- an awesome challenge; one which the government was sure could not be met. Amtrak was created to buy time for the American passenger train to die a dignified death.

ABOVE: The Amtrak *Broadway Limited* rips through Cornwells Heights on the final leg of its journey from Chicago with a long consist during a pleasant spring morning in April, 1974.

LEFT: Amtrak 41-- the westbound *Broadway*-- slows for a North Philadelphia station stop on a warm evening in July, 1975.

Two photos/William J. Coxey

LEFT: During Amtrak's early years, the Washington D.C. section of the *Broadway Limited* operated between Harrisburg and Washington via the former PRR Columbia & Port Deposit electrified freight line, following the east shore of the Susquehanna River from Harrisburg, Pennsylvania to Perryville, Maryland. The eastward (Washington-bound) *Broadway* is seen along the Susquehanna south of Columbia, PA on April 23, 1973.

BELOW: A diesel-powered *Broadway Limited* Washington section is seen at Pequea on the former PRR Port Road in June, 1972. Note Union Pacific coach in consist; Amtrak was but one year into repainting its fleet into its own livery. An Amtrak sleeper-lounge-observation brings up the markers.

Two Kodachromes/Tom Nemeth

On May 1, 1971, a radical change came about in the routes, number of trains, and types of equipment operated by most of the nation's railroads. The first day of service under Amtrak saw many passenger trains and routes gone forever. The new system, however, created some new and interesting routes: *The Broadway Limited* was retained under the new system and a new Washington section was added, operating between Washington and Harrisburg over the electrified, former-PRR Port Road, a route which hadn't seen a passenger train in years. The Pennsylvania Railroad had operated its Washington-Harrisburg connections via York over the Northern Central Railroad

Amtrak selected the best remaining passenger equipment from the participating railroads. It was not unusual to see eastern

ABOVE: The photographer raced 150 miles from Lanesboro to Harrisburg, PA just in time to catch a matched set of A-B-A Amtrak E8's arriving with a twelve-minute late eastbound *Broadway Limited* on October 29, 1978.
Kodachrome/Denis E. Connell

BELOW: The engine change at Harrisburg offered enough time to hop off the *Broadway* and walk up to the head end to take a picture. The photographer found a mixed set of A-B-A-A Amtrak E8's on the point during a westbound vacation trip on July 27, 1979.
Kodachrome/Denis E. Connell

ABOVE: Eastbound *Broadway Limited* rounds the curve at Newport, PA on April 29, 1978 with an interesting F40PH/E8B/E8A lashup.
Kodachrome/David Hill

BELOW: A few miles east, the *Broadway* rolls past the former PRR station in Duncannon, PA behind twin F40PH's in June, 1984.
Kodachrome/Denis E. Connell

trains with Southern Pacific, Union Pacific and Santa Fe equipment still in its original paint schemes. This mixing of equipment created some colorful consists in Amtrak's early years, but it wasn't long before Amtrak painted these colorful cars in its standard platinum mist scheme.

In 1974 Amtrak refurbished and renamed several 8 roomette-6 double bedroom Rock Island sleepers for *Broadway Limited* service.

The cars refurbished and renamed included the following, courtesy Robert J. Wayner's *Amtrak Car and Locomotive Spotter, 3rd Edition*:

Amtrak 2551 *Times Square*
ex-CRI&P car 631 - *The Broadmoor*

Amtrak 2552 *Brooklyn Bridge*
ex-CRI&P car 632 - *Rampart Range*

Amtrak 2553 *Central Park*
ex-CRI&P car 633 - *Turquoise Sky*

Amtrak 2554 *Golden Triangle*
ex-CRI&P car 634 - *Lake Nokomis*

Amtrak 2555 *Steel City*
ex-CRI&P car 635 - *Buffalo Bayou*

Amtrak 2556 *The Potomac*
ex-CRI&P car 636 - *San Jacinto*

Amtrak 2557 *Cherry Blossom*
ex-CRI&P car *Golden Horizon*

Amtrak 2558 *Rock Creek*
ex-CRI&P car *Golden Journey*

Amtrak 2559 *Windy City*
ex-CRI&P car *Golden Meadow*

Amtrak 2560 *Wrigley Field*
ex-CRI&P car 637 - *Golden Spire*

Amtrak 2561 *Lincoln Park*
ex-CRI&P car 638 - *Golden Tower*

For patriotic reasons, ex-CRI&P car 630 retained its original name, *Air Force Academy*, renumbered Amtrak 2550.

Some of these cars are now in Mexico.

While Amtrak began purchasing new passenger cars and motive power, some of the railroads either refused to give Amtrak trains priority over freight trains or failed to maintain their roadbeds in optimum condition for the operation of fast passenger trains. In Amtrak's *Broadway Limited* schedule of October 26, 1975, Amtrak made the following apology to passengers:

Note: The above schedules are considerably slower than the Penn Central is required to provide under its contract with Amtrak. However, while work progresses to overcome deteriorated track conditions, faster schedules are impossible to achieve at this time.

The October 26, 1975 schedule listed *The Broadway* leaving New York at 4:55 P.M. and arriving in Chicago at 10:35 A.M. In 1951 *The Broadway* left New York at 6:00 P.M. and arrived in Chicago at 9:00 A.M.

In 1975 Amtrak changed the routing of the Washington section of *The Broadway*. The Port Deposit route along the Susquehanna River was dropped in favor of running the section via the Northeast Corridor to 30th Street Station, Philadelphia, thence westward via Lancaster to Harrisburg. The Washington section was combined with the New York section at Harrisburg.

The circuitous routing via 30th Street was not satisfactory, and on October 1, 1981 a new routing and a new name for the Washington-Chicago section was inaugurated. This new routing operated over the B&O (Chessie System) between Washington and Pittsburgh and the name of the train was changed to the *Capitol Limited*. There was a certain irony in this because *The Capitol Limited* with its improved connections via trackage rights over the P&LE in the 1930's was in part responsible for the demise of PRR's Washington-Chicago *Liberty Limited*. Under Amtrak the new *Capitol Limited* was combined with the *Broadway Limited* at Pittsburgh for the westward run to Chicago.

The first eastward trip of *The Capitol Limited* from Pittsburgh included F40's 275 and 305, two baggage cars, slumbercoach 2086, former Santa Fe coaches 4711 and 4702, and cafeteria-lounge 3124. Car 3124 was formerly the *Betsy Ross*, which had once been a 29-seat/1-drawing room parlor car assigned to *The Congressional* trains built by Budd for the PRR in 1952. Quite ironic: A car from PRR's former premier train on the New York-Washington run and the archrival of B&O's *Royal Blue*, running on the *Capitol Limited* which connected with *The Broadway Limited*.

The Amtrak system timetable of April 27, 1986 showed the Washington-Pittsburgh running time of *The Capitol Limited* as seven hours and fifteen minutes. This running time was two hours and fifteen minutes faster than the previous routing via 30th Street.

With the schedule change of October 26, 1986, Amtrak began operating *The Broadway* and *Capitol* as two separate trains, eliminating the combined consist between Pittsburgh to Chicago. This separate operation allowed Amtrak to increase the number of mail and passenger cars that could be efficiently handled on each train. Prior to the establishment of separate consists west of Pittsburgh, the combined train was handling 16 to 18 cars; the maximum that could be operated. As a result of the separate operation, each train increased the number of mail cars and *The Capitol* was assigned a full diner.

TOP PHOTO: Amtrak train 40, the eastbound *Broadway Limited* completes its station work at Lancaster, Pennsylvania at 7:43 A.M. May 11, 1974. GG1 920 is in charge of the 12-car consist.
  Kodachrome/Robert Malinoski

RIGHT: The Washington, D.C. section of the *Broadway* was changed from a Port Road routing to operation via Philadelphia (30th Street) and the Northeast Corridor by the mid-1970's. GG1 4939 wheels the Washington-bound *Broadway* through Marcus Hook, PA on the Corridor, December 28, 1975.
  Kodachrome/David L. Hill

AMTRAK *Broadway Limited* dinner menu from 1976. The bill of fare is substantial. Note Amtrak's acceptance of major credit cards one of the rail company's customer service enhancements made to improve dining car service. And that traditional *Broadway Limited* New York strip steak is still offered, costing but $7.95....

Perry Billington collection

Good Evening

Please write your dinner order on the meal check.

A la Carte

Appetizers

Chilled Fruit Juice....45   Soup of the Day....55   Fruit Cup....75

Beefburger Deluxe

Onion Slice, Tomato
Garnished with Potato Chips
1.85

Cheeseburger Deluxe

1.95

Ham Steak with Raisin Sauce

Potato & Vegetable
Dinner Rolls & Butter
3.25

Short Ribs of Beef

Potato & Vegetable
Dinner Rolls & Butter
3.95

Desserts

Apple Pie....65   Blueberry Pie....65
with Cheese or a la Mode....75   or a la Mode....75
Ice Cream with Chocolate Sauce....55   Baked Apple....50

Beverages

Pot of Coffee, Sanka or Hot Tea....40; Cup....25
Glass of Milk....30; Iced Tea....25

Beverage List

FROM THE BAR — 1.50

SCOTCH	MARTINI (GIN)
BOURBON	MARTINI (VODKA)
CANADIAN	MANHATTAN
VODKA	OLD FASHIONED
GIN	DAIQUIRI
RUM	WHISKEY SOUR
COCKTAIL SHERRY	

MIXES
GINGER ALE   TONIC WATER   CLUB SODA
BLOODY MARY   ORANGE JUICE
COCA COLA   SEVEN UP

BEER
BEER...ALE....75
PREMIUM BEER....90

Wine with your meal

Selected White, Rosé and Red
Wines are available for your
dining enjoyment.
(2.00 Half Bottle)

CORDIALS...1.50
COGNAC   DRAMBUIE
CREME DE MENTHE
CREAM SHERRY

SOFT DRINKS....40
COCA COLA   GINGER ALE   SEVEN UP
SPRITE   FRESCA   TAB

A Broadway Favorite

BROILED 12 oz. NEW YORK STRIP STEAK
(TOP CHOICE U.S.D.A. BEEF)

Mushroom Caps

Baked or Creamy Whipped Potatoes

Vegetable or Green Salad

Dinner Rolls   Beverage

$7.95

Table d'Hote

Price of entree is price of complete dinner.

Choice of: Chilled Fruit Juice; Soup of the Day; Fruit Cup

Entrees

Served with our Crock of Cheese & Relish Caddy
Roast Sirloin of Beef, au Jus...6.50
Filet of Sole, with Lemon Butter...4.50
Cheese Omelette...3.75
Rock Cornish Game Hen...4.75
Green Garden Salad with Choice of Dressing:
French, Bleu Cheese, Thousand Island
Creamy Whipped Potatoes or Parslied Potatoes
Assorted Vegetables   Dinner Rolls & Butter

Desserts

Apple Pie   Blueberry Pie
Ice Cream with Chocolate Sauce

Beverages

Coffee   Tea   Milk   Sanka
After Dinner Mints

Menu Prices Include All State and Local Taxes
MAJOR CREDIT CARDS ACCEPTED

LEFT: Amtrak GG1 4935, restored to its earlier splendor through the efforts of Friends of the GG1 (FOGG) arrives at Harrisburg station with the *Broadway Limited* on its 75th Anniversary Run, June 15, 1977.
Kodachrome/Don Jilson

BELOW: Photographers get their pictures of GG1 4935 upon arrival at the Harrisburg station on the 75th Anniversary run of the *Broadway Limited*.
Photo/Homer R. Hill

HAPPY BIRTHDAY BROADWAY

On June 15, 1977 Amtrak celebrated the 75th Anniversary of its famed *Broadway Limited*. Actually, the event involved some juggling of history, since the *Broadway Limited* name wasn't in use until 1912. But June 15, 1902 did mark the beginning of the Great Competition between the Pennsylvania and New York Central Railroads; for on that date the Pennsy renamed and recast its *Pennsylvania Limited* into a new and faster *Pennsylvania Special*, running on a *Century*-competitive 20-hour New York-Chicago schedule.

TOP LEFT: *Broadway Limited* tail sign, taped to the rear of Amtrak observation lounge car 3341 on the 75th Anniversary Run of the *Broadway Limited*.
Kodachrome/Don Jilson.
TOP RIGHT: Amtrak mustered a perfectly matched, freshly painted set of A-B-B-A E8's to the take 75th Anniversary Run consist west from Harrisburg on June 15, 1977.
Kodachrome/Don Jilson
BELOW: *Broadway Limited* 75th Anniversary Cake, baked specially for the 75th Anniversary Run. Train passengers from New York and Philadelphia were treated to a slice and a sip of champagne enroute to Harrisburg.
Photo/Homer R. Hill

Restored GG1 4935 in Pennsylvania Railroad livery hauled Amtrak's *Broadway* west from Pennsylvania Station, New York City to Harrisburg with a cadre of invited guests and dignitaries aboard to toast the occasion. A large *Broadway* birthday cake was prominently displayed in the diner, and before arrival at Harrisburg the onboard guests had been offered the opportunity to enjoy a slice.

Amtrak had planned ahead for the big event, and waiting at Harrisburg was a freshly-painted matched set of A-B-B-A E8's waiting to rush the train westward over the Alleghenies. A final touch of class; a round-end observation car brought up the markers, replete with a *Broadway Limited* tail sign.

The eastbound *Broadway Limited* **slows for the station stop at Huntingdon, Pennsylvania on the Pennsy's formerly four-track Middle Division, July 28, 1984. HUNT tower, now closed, is visible at right. As the only schedule between New York and Chicago, the Broadway still services the smaller towns in Central Pennsylvania including Lewistown and Huntington.**

Photo/Alex Mayes

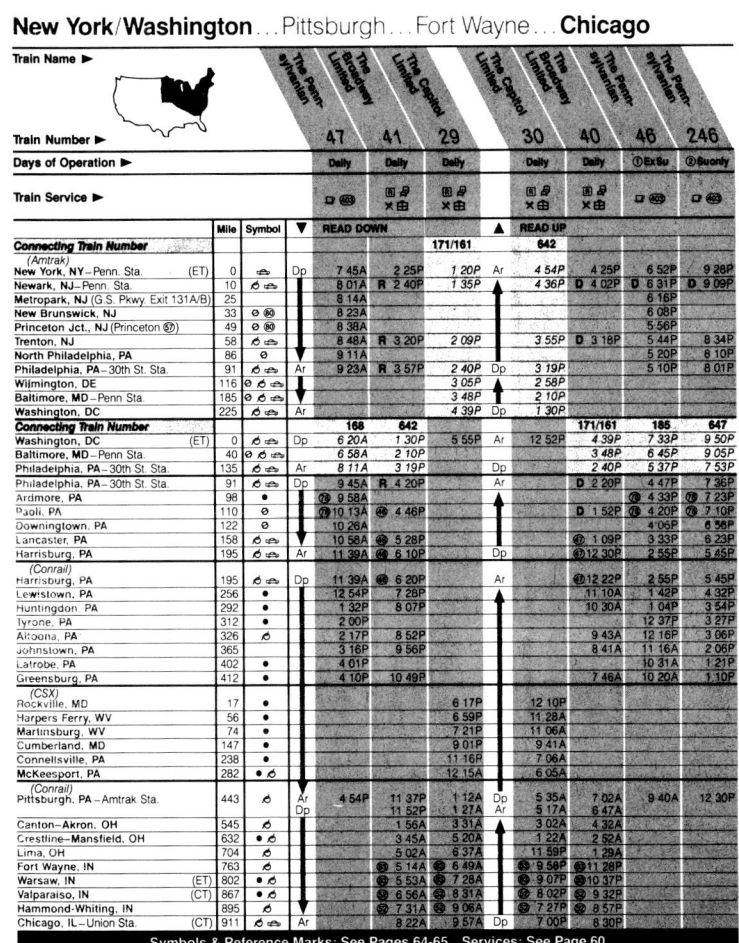

Amtrak 40 barrels through Bryn Mawr on the famous Pennsy "Main Line", running 20 minutes late on a Saturday afternoon in November, 1982.

Photo/William J. Coxey

ALL ABOARD THE BROADWAY LIMITED: Amtrak timetable effective September 18, 1988 through January 14, 1989 provides the most recent *Broadway Limited* schedule. Note that Amtrak now shows *Broadway Limited* and *Capitol Limited* service in a combined schedule. *Broadway* and *Capitol* operate as separate trains through to Chicago; they are no longer combined and split at Pittsburgh.

Amtrak continues to improve its nationwide network, and the *Broadway Limited* continues to provide daily first class service between New York City and Chicago. In the mid-1980's the *Broadway* received a new head-end-power consist, improving mechanical reliability and passenger comfort. The train now serves 30th Street Station in Philadelphia on its New York-Chicago route: An electric locomotive hauls the trainset backwards between New York City and 30th Street, where the motor is cut off and F40PH diesels are attached to the rear (which then becomes the head end) for the run west via Lancaster. Harrisburg is no longer a locomotive change point, nor are cars switched in and out of the consist there.

The *Broadway* no longer carries an observation car nor a twin-unit diner, and such luxuries as an on-board barbershop and Master Room accommodations are but pleasant memories. But Trains 40 and 41 do carry the flag on Amtrak's most famous New York-Chicago route.

LEFT: Amtrak 40, the eastbound *Broadway Limited*, has Conrail U25B 2635 assisting Amtrak E8's 427, 451 and 440 on a 16-car consist at Barree, Pennsylvania 10:50 A.M. May 14, 1977. Train has just emerged from Spruce Creek Tunnel, out of view around curve.
Kodachrome/Robert Malinoski

FACING PAGE: The *Broadway Limited* rounds the most famous landmark on its Chicago to New York route-- Horseshoe Curve-- six miles west of Altoona, Pennsylvania, on May 14, 1977.
Kodachrome/Tom Nemeth

RIGHT: Three Amtrak E8A's, running "elephant style" bring the *Broadway* down the hill into Altoona at Milepost 241 at 10:18 A.M. May 16, 1977. E8 412 is in charge of the 15-car consist.
Kodachrome/Robert Malinoski

BROADWAY LIMITED

WASHINGTON, D.C./
NEW YORK-CHICAGO

Welcome aboard Amtrak's
BROADWAY LIMITED

...the famed glamour train from the great Eastern cities to the mighty Midwest.

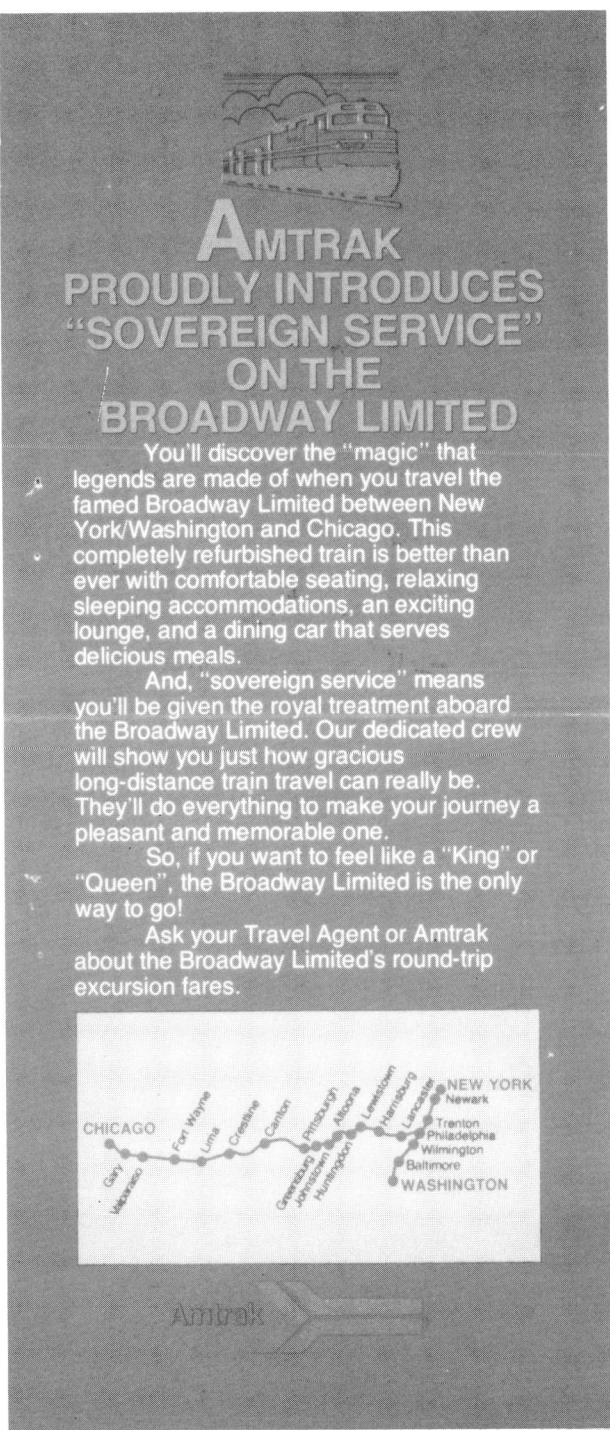

BROADWAY PROMOTIONS

AMTRAK CONTINUES THE TRADITION of making the Broadway Limited the New York-Chicago flagship. Descriptive Broadway Limited route brochures, pictured on opposite page, were produced and distributed to on-baord passengers. Pictured are guides from 1975 and 1977. The '75 guide at far left includes a fold-out full color Rand McNally road map with the route of the Broadway overprinted in red.

Pictured on this page is an advertising card and large button touting "Sovereign Service", from a recent Amtrak Broadway Limited promotion.

Tom Gallo collection

ABOVE: Amtrak SDP40-F 588 leads the westbound *Broadway Limited* upgrade around the famed Horseshoe Curve in the gathering dusk in May, 1976. Photographs of the westbound *Broadway* on Horseshoe are few, as it has traditionally passed this point well after dark.

Kodachrome/Jim Boyd

ABOVE: Amtrak F40PH 327 leads the eastbound *Broadway Limited* around Horseshoe Curve with a long consist on May 27, 1980.

Kodachrome/Don Jilson

RIGHT: The eastbound *Broadway* pauses for station work and a new crew at Pittsburgh in March, 1977. Freight units such as the ones at left often served as helpers out of Pittsburgh for the eastward climb to the summit at Cresson.

Kodachrome/Jim Boyd

THE VIEW FROM ROOSEVELT ROAD:

TOP LEFT: Amtrak SDP40F's 590 and 597 lead the eastbound *Broadway Limited* out of Chicago Union Station, March 21, 1976. Kodachrome/Preston Cook

LEFT: Two months later, E units substituted for the troublesome SDP40F's on this *Broadway Limited* trip of May 22, 1976. Kodachrome/Preston Cook

ABOVE: A pair of F40PH's and head-end powered Heritage coaches comprise the *Broadway* consist on May 21, 1981. Kodachrome/Denis E. Connell

REFERENCES

Beebe, Lucius,
   20TH CENTURY,
   Howell-North, Berkeley, 1962.

Burgess, George and Miles C. Kennedy,
   CENTENNIAL HISTORY OF THE
   PENNSYLVANIA RAILROAD
   COMPANY 1846-1946.
   The Pennsylvania R.R. Co.,
   Philadelphia, 1949.

Cupper, Dan, *A Capitol Idea,*
   PASSENGER TRAIN JOURNAL,
   December 1981.

Dubin, Arthur D.,
   MORE CLASSIC TRAINS,
   Kalmbach Publishing Co.,
   Milwaukee, 1974.

Dubin, Arthur D.,
   SOME CLASSIC TRAINS,
   Kalmbach Publishing Co.,
   Milwaukee, 1964.

Hollander, Ron,
   ALL ABOARD (The Lionel Story),
   Workman Publishing Company,
   New York, 1981.

Kratville, William W.,
   STEAM, STEEL & LIMITEDS,
   Kratville Publications, 1962.

NEW YORK TIMES
   Affairs of Railroads, October 29, 1881.
   Pennsylvania's Fast-Train, June 16, 1902.
   Twentieth Century Flier, June 16, 1902.
   8 Hours to Chicago By Pennsylvania
     Flyer, June 3, 1905.
   Fast Chicago Trains Are To Run Slower,
     November 9, 1912.
   Twenty Hours Fast Enough, November 10, 1912.
   New Chicago Train Has Preview Run, June 9, 1938.
   Streamline Trains Hailed In First Run,
     June 17, 1938.
   The 20th Century Makes Final Run,
     December 3, 1967.
   Broadway Limited Ends 65-Year Run From
     Penn Station, December 13, 1967.
   Penn Central Seeks To Abandon N.Y.-Chicago
     Passenger Runs, March 5, 1970.

RAILWAY AGE,
   Pullman Builds New Equipment,
   June 18, 1938.

Vranich, Joseph,
   Which Way For The Broadway Limited,
   PASSENGER TRAIN JOURNAL,
   April 1981.

Wayner, Robert J.,
   CAR NAMES, NUMBERS AND CONSISTS,
   Wayner Publications, 1972.
Wayner, Robert J.,
   THE COMPLETE ROSTER OF
   HEAVYWEIGHT PULLMAN CARS,
   Wayner Publications, 1985.

Westing, Fred,
   PENNSY STEAM AND SEMAPHORES,
   Bonanza Books, 1982.

Woods, Katherine,
   The Broadway Limited,
   THE MUTUAL MAGAZINE, June 1929.

Wornom, Douglas,
   HISTORY: PASSENGER TRAIN AND
   THROUGH CAR SERVICE
   PENNSYLVANIA RAILROAD 1849-1947,
   Published by D. Wornom,
   Dist. by Owen Davies, Bookseller, Chicago, 1974.

ACKNOWLEDGEMENTS

The authors extend their appreciation to the following for their generous assistance:

Charles A. Brown
Alley Bertsch
Perry Billington
Jim Boyd
Robert F. Collins
Denis E. Connell
Preston Cook
William J. Coxey
Larry Fischer
Richard D. Forest
David L. Hill
Homer Hill
Jean Hill
Don Jilson
Tom Kelcec
Stan Kistler
Robert Lewis of *Railway Age Magazine*
Bill Longo
Bob Lorenz
Bob Malinoski
Alex Mayes
John McCall
Howard B. Morris
National Railway Publication Company
   Publishers of *The Official Railway Guide*
Tom Nemeth
E. Lewis Pardee
Mike Schafer of *Passenger Train Journal*
Alvin Siebold - *Pullman Classics Limited*
Smithsonian Institution,
   Office of Printing and Photographic Services
George E. Votava
Robert J. Wayner of *Wayner Publications*
Martin S. Zak

Meet the Authors

This is the fourth book which Joel and Tom have co-authored. Three of their books have been published by Railpace Company: *The Seashore's Finest Train, Iron Horses Across the Garden State,* and their latest work, *Broadway Limited.* Joel and Tom also co-authored with Don Wood *The Unique New York & Long Branch,* published by Audio-Visual Designs.

Joel Rosenbaum is a graduate of Brookdale Community College and Rutgers University, and a Viet Nam veteran, having served with the United States Air Force. He is a member of the Pennsylvania Railroad Technical & Historical Society, New Haven Railroad Historical and Technical Association, and the Jersey Central Chapter, NRHS. Joel is employed as a Registered Respiratory Therapist at a large Monmouth County, New Jersey hospital.

TOM GALLO

JOEL ROSENBAUM

Joel Rosenbaum and Tom Gallo have been interested in the Pennsylvania Railroad and its passenger trains from their earliest years. Joel grew up in Linden, New Jersey, two blocks from the Pennsy's six-track Broad Way and the local station. Joel's father was a regular Pennsy commuter to New York. Daily father and son greetings at the railroad station were often followed by admiring glances as the *Broadway Limited* roared through town on its westward journey to Chicago.

One of Tom Gallo's uncles was a Pennsy engineer. This "in" was Tom's passport to cab rides in GG1 electrics and E8 diesels. Tom has collected passenger train memorabilia of the Pennsylvania Railroaad from the turn of the century through the Penn Central merger.

Tom Gallo is a graduate of Keyport High School, and is a veteran of the United States Army Engineer Corps. Tom is a member of the Railroadians, The Keyport Historical Society, and the Jersey Central Chapter, NRHS. He is employed by NJ Transit, serving as Terminal Supervisor of Pennsylvania Station, Newark, New Jersey.

BROADWAY REBORN: *Broadway Limited* sleeper-lounge-observation *Mountain View* has been acquired and restored by Pullman Classics Limited of Glen Rock, New Jersey. *Mountain View* is seen in Chicago on May 30, 1988 prior to its move east to New Jersey. Soon it will again, on occasion, bring up markers on Amtrak 41-- the *Broadway Limited*.
Kodachrome/Alvin R. Siebold-Pullman Classics Limited